Her Majesty The Queen, Parliament Square, 19 November 2007.

The Story of the Jubilee Walkway & the Jubilee Greenway

A Walk for
The Queen

HUGO VICKERS

First published in 2012 by The Dovecote Press Ltd
Stanbridge, Wimborne Minster, Dorset BH21 4JD
in association with The Jubilee Walkway Trust

ISBN 978-1-904-34999-0
Text © Hugo Vickers 2012
Photographs © The Jubilee Walkway Trust

Designed by The Dovecote Press
Printed and bound in Singapore by KHL Printing Pte Ltd

All papers used by The Dovecote Press are natural,
recyclable products made from wood grown in sustainable,
well-managed forests

A CIP catalogue record for this book is available
from the British Library

1 3 5 7 9 8 6 4 2

Contents

Foreword

HIS ROYAL HIGHNESS THE DUKE OF GLOUCESTER

KENSINGTON PALACE
LONDON W8 4PU

I have greatly enjoyed being associated with the Jubilee Walkway since its imaginative creation in 1977. It has been exciting to see it develop, in particular opening up the route along the South Bank of the Thames, now such a vibrant part of London life. The Walkway encourages people to walk and cycle and the panoramic panels interpret the views, many of them concentrating on interesting architectural features; encouraging the view that the walker or cyclist is in the right place at the right time.

As this book shows, the Trust has passed through many phases, some more active than others. But since the Golden Jubilee in 2002, the Trust received a great boost leading to the creation of the 60 kilometre Jubilee Greenway to celebrate The Queen's Diamond Jubilee and unite the various Olympic sites including many more parts of London. One day in 2009, most enjoyably, we explored the Stratford part of that route on bicycles in the early days of its creation.

This book tells the story of the two routes and could well prove to be a useful handbook to others who embark on such imaginative ambitions.

Introduction

This is a story that began with the vision of a man who declared that he had 'been unwise enough to get mixed up' in a great number of affairs. Max Nicholson was a largely unsung visionary, variously an ornithologist, environmentalist and a leading figure in the 1951 Festival of Britain. He was happy to admit to being 'impatient, irascible and hypercritical', but he was also a dreamer, a conciliator and a healer of dissension. He dreamt up the Jubilee Walkway.

He and his successors had many battles to wage. These they tended to win by refusing to be deterred by adverse circumstance and by employing a kind of Quixotic enthusiasm in all their endeavours. For the Jubilee Walkway was fortunate to be run by a succession of Trustees who brought to it their own individual enthusiasm, their tenacity, their knowledge of architecture and planning issues, but above all their Max-like vision. 'We were a bunch of amiable lunatics,' recalled Joyce Bellamy, the long-serving honorary Secretary.

This book concerns a route round London – in fact two routes round London. I have studied the reports, the files and the memoranda, but I hope to have gone beyond that, relying on diaries, personal interviews and observation. There have been successes and failures and I hope to have reflected this. There has even been tragedy – I have included the saga in which one of the Trustees was murdered, his body chopped up, sawed in the bath and incinerated. His murderer was convicted without the body being found. Perhaps this will encourage the casual reader to read on?

Any successful enterprise is a tribute to the cunning manoeuvres of its creators. I was not the creator of the Walkway. I am the inheritor, the lucky person to preside over a fabulous phase in which it seems that everything we have wanted has fallen into our laps. The pioneering work was done by others, and

ABOVE Max Nicholson.

OPPOSITE PAGE Canary Wharf from the Jubilee Greenway.

reading the files, I see how hard they worked. I have not had to fund raise or go to planning meetings. During my phase as Chairman, I have been lucky to have the support of Jim Walker, who has pulled rabbit after rabbit out of many different hats, and also to have enjoyed the benefits of the wisdom of the surviving Trustees, one of whom was there at the start and many of whom were involved in moulding the concept of the Walkway from its earliest days.

Forgive a personal introduction. Just as many of the key figures of the Silver Jubilee were Festival of Britain men, I came to be involved through the Windsor Festival and working with Kate Trevelyan in 1974. She went on to be administrator of the

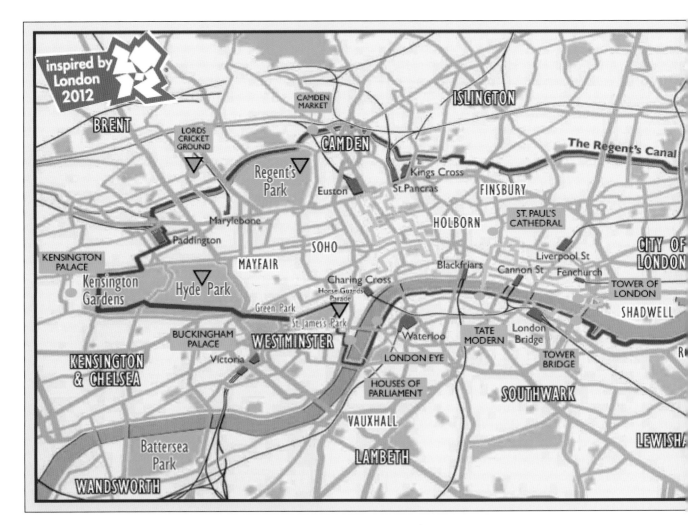

LEFT Kate Trevelyan.

London Celebrations Committee for The Queen's Silver Jubilee and in due course invited me to join her team. I was also involved with the Commemorative Collectors' Society and we were staging an exhibition for the 1977 Silver Jubilee. A group of us collectors went along to see John Denison, who was to run the Cultural Committee. We saw him on 14 May 1976. I recorded the encounter in my diary:

> A meeting with John Denison, the ex-Director of the Festival Hall. Now he is in charge of the Silver Jubilee [Cultural] Committee for London. A tall, friendly man, a big fellow, a keen musician, and the sort of person who clearly knows everyone. Steven Jackson, Henry Wollaston and I were there to talk about a Commemorative Collectors exhibition at the

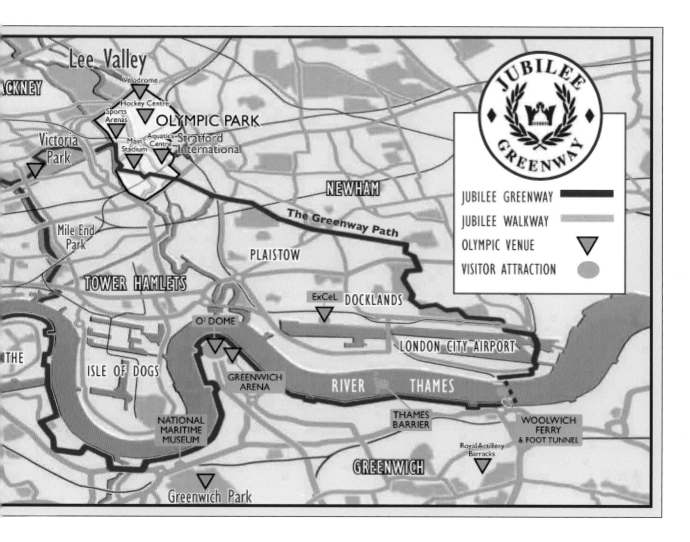

Royal Exchange for next year. He identified Henry's father by his musical activities in an orchestra in Deal and then later confirmed this by stating 'And he was Garter.' [Sir Gerald Woods Wollaston].

If he agreed with you, John Denison smiled warmly. If not, then his face looked up to the ceiling and he squashed up his mouth. This meant he didn't. A compromise was reached and he smiled again.

Amongst things he told us – he said that as Director of the Royal Festival Hall he was often rung up by Robert Armstrong, Heath's Private Secretary to ask if he could slip the P.M. in to the 2nd act of this or that. He did his best. The meeting was a success.

A few weeks later, on 15 June, on the strength of the exhibition idea, I was invited to the launch of the London Celebrations Committee at the Banqueting House in Whitehall. This group had come together spontaneously to help Londoners celebrate The Queen's Silver Jubilee. I wish I could repeat the message given to us in speeches and documentation but my diary is, once again, merely gossip:

I went along to the Reception for the London Committee for the Silver Jubilee. I was received by Lord Drogheda, and then found I knew no one, but not for long, as presently there was Jeffrey Daniels, who is putting on an exhibition called 'Lousy but Loyal' in the East End. Dreadful name – I expect it will be just that!

Kate [Trevelyan] came up & we had a long chat, in fact stayed together for the rest of the evening. We talked about the [Windsor] Festival.... Ian Hunter was there, and Colonel [Johnnie]

Johnston. Kit Aston loomed in his massive form – Keith Jeffrey smiled over the room [These were all Windsor Festival figures. Ian Hunter created it, Sir John Johnston represented the Lord Chamberlain's Office, Sir Christopher Aston was Mayor of Windsor, and Keith Jeffrey was the Arts Council representative].

More interesting were talks with John Denison – he'd been in the choir of St George's under Sir Walter Parratt [organist of the Chapel], who couldn't use his little fingers, but made up for it with pedals, who'd play chess on one side out of his head – and listen to Test Match scores or whatever on the other. He was encouraging about the Royal Exchange . . . [Our exhibition, *Jubilee Royal*, was finally staged at Goldsmiths' Hall, and opened by Princess Alice, Duchess of Gloucester].

We talked to Sir Hugh Casson, who has designed a new [Windsor] Festival cover. Sir Harold Wilson and the Duke of Grafton had just been installed as Knights of the Garter and had walked side by side in the procession. He wants to do Harold Wilson in a Gannex-lined Garter mantle with Hugh Grafton looming above him! He has a way of clasping one as he speaks – both Kate and me.

In February 1977 Kate Trevelyan invited me to come and work for the London Celebrations Committee. My job was to sell flags. Thus instead of shuffling round London looking at my feet, I looked up towards the roofs of buildings to see if they had a flagpole. I am not a good salesman by nature but I had the idea to give a flag to Apsley House. This was very widely seen at Hyde Park Corner, from both Piccadilly and Park Lane, and encouraged others to buy it. I plodded round hotels and offices and was sometimes successful in getting them to place orders. It was hard in March, but became easier as Jubilee fever mounted. I also worked out which way my bosses, Lord Drogheda, Jeffrey Sterling and Sir Paul Wright were driven to work and made a point of targeting the flagpoles along those routes.

I started work on 16 February. It was hard to extract the flags from the dismal Mr Huggins of Black & Edgington who proved unable to cope with the orders. I wanted 300 flags and 60 banners. On 12 April I told Kate Trevelyan that Huggins could not cope with our order and that I should probably give up and go home. The solution was to collect the existing flags and sell them direct from the office at 4 Carlton Gardens. I recall driving back from the factory in Sidcup, my car stuffed with flags from top to bottom. I could not see out of the back window.

These flags had various uses during Jubilee year. David Hamilton, Ceremonial Officer at the GLC, rang me one day and asked for one for the great flagpole on the South Bank near the newly created Jubilee Gardens. Illtyd Harrington, Deputy Leader of the GLC, was to hoist this flag. David was delighted when I arrived with a huge blue one with a white crown on it, though he joked that Illtyd, a Labour man, would certainly have preferred a red one.

David also called me when banners were needed for the unveiling of the Jubilee Walkway and the opening of the Jubilee Gardens by The Queen. He rang late on the Friday before the Bank Holiday weekend in June, the unveiling being scheduled for the following Tuesday. I was going to a wedding that weekend, but found a haberdasher's shop in Chester where I purchased some suitable trims. The friends I stayed with on the Saturday were slightly surprised to see me spending every free moment sewing them on. By the Tuesday two flags had become banners, duly used by The Queen.

In the meantime Kate gave me two new jobs. The first was to keep a record of the Jubilee as it developed and the second was to help sell the official guidebook for the Silver Jubilee Walkway. So I date my involvement with the Walkway to 12 April 1977.

The plan was to get these guidebooks distributed. This involved working with Anne Dillon, who was employed by the Environmental Committee, run by Max Nicholson. There was always a chance that this little book, devised by Max, would be taken over by a large distributor, but in the meantime there was nothing to be done but go out onto the route and try to persuade outlets to stock it. The book itself was still no more than a mock-up proof. On a Saturday afternoon we set off to walk the mapped out route:

We drove to Leicester Square where we established the starting-point of the Walkway and then approached one or two people – a woman in a shop and an 'itinerant vendor' in the square. It was rather

The Jubilee flag is hoisted in Jubilee Gardens, 1977.

successful, but this was the limit of our achievement. After that we drove to Victoria Tower Gardens and inspected the Queen's oak and a plaque and I had a look at the English version of the Burghers of Calais. Anne bought ice creams and we sat by the river on a glorious, sunny afternoon.

From there we went to the Jubilee Gardens on the South Bank which are progressing well. We saw the men at work and I learned of some more of the problems. It is a very windy spot so walls have been built. Apparently it will definitely be ready by that famous date, 9 June. Thence to the [William Curtis] Ecological Park [today Potter's Fields] by HMS *Belfast* which was also the scene of activity. Some were working harder than others. I understand they all do so voluntarily and spend the whole weekend at work. What one must also remember is that the finished product is newly sewn grass and spindly trees, not Kew Gardens!

Following that we went aboard HMS *Belfast*, where we were given a conducted tour by a man in charge who took a great shine to Anne Dillon. We ended our afternoon in the bar of the ship, and re-reading this account many years later, I am forced to wonder how effective we were as a selling team.

The following Monday W.H. Smith Distributors took 50,000 copies of the programme for £20,000. It was the easy way out but I was disappointed thinking we could have made the Trust £32,000 by dint of our door-to-door activities. Thereafter my job was confined to confirming orders – 100 guides to the Victoria & Albert Museum and GLC bookshop, 10 to Westminster Abbey etc. As it turned out, W.H. Smith did not do a good job. They sold very few and devoted minimal effort to promotion. In February 1978 they asked for £10,000 for the return of the unsold copies. The Walkway Trust agreed to offer £3,000.

On 26 April there was a reception at the Swiss Centre at which Dr W. Kaempfen, Director of the Swiss National Tourist Office, welcomed the new Silver Jubilee Walkway which, as he said in his

Launch of the Clean Up London Campaign.

speech 'allowed visitors to discover the beauty of London, while, at the same time, improving their health.' To help walkers on their way, all the 100 guests were presented with walking sticks, decorated for the occasion. I still have mine.

The VIPS were given specially created ones – The Lord Mayor of Westminster, a dedicated cyclist, got one with a wheel, lamp, brake and bell. Air Commodore Innes accepted one for the Lord Lieutenant (Marshal of the RAF Lord Elworthy) designed to ensure 'a flying start to the journey.' Lord Drogheda's was adorned with a ballerina's skirt and dancing slippers, which infuriated him since he was an opera man, not a ballet man; that of Lord Ponsonby of Shulbrede, Chairman of the GLC, was adorned with cleaning materials in tribute to his 'Clean Up London' campaign. Amongst other recipients, Max Nicholson was given one decorated with feathered birds.

In the windows of the Swiss Centre were other walking sticks – a motorised one for the faint-

hearted, an illuminated one for after-dark strollers, and a rather curious one for the Swiss version of the city gent – with a bow tie and a furled umbrella. Meanwhile the Silver Jubilee Walkway was scheduled for completion on 30 May, albeit with some way-marking to be done and other work still in progress.

After 26 April my first brief association with the Jubilee Walkway was over. Instead I was assigned further tasks – to help arrange the visits of The Duke of Gloucester to open Portobello Green and Princess Anne to open Newham City Farm, the first of several such endeavours. This was to prove good experience for arranging later royal visits, though at the time, both these sites were under development. 'We'll walk the Duke of Gloucester through the mud and battle through the chickens with Princess Anne,' was my comment at the time. Meanwhile the flags sold like hot cakes.

Views of the Jubilee Gardens in 1977 when it was still a carpark, during its original construction, during the course of it being redesigned in 2012, and finally finished.

The Origins of the Jubilee Walkway

A Jubilee is a celebration and a Walkway is a route to walk. The Silver Jubilee Walkway (as it was originally called) emerged as a permanent memorial to the celebrations marking the Silver Jubilee of Queen Elizabeth II in 1977. Since then it has lived through many phases. It led to the complete rejuvenation of the South Bank, a process which took many years to complete and ended eventually in the creation of The Queen's Walk. It pushed its way through a number of areas of London. Panoramic panels were introduced to interpret the views and the changing nature of the skyline of London. In 2002, to mark the Golden Jubilee, it was completely restored and revamped, the panels upgraded and in many cases replaced.

Over the years the Walkway has provided an opportunity for trees to be planted and benches to be put in strategic and opportune places in London.

The Queen and The Duke of Edinburgh unveiling the Parliament Square panoramic panel, 19 November 2007, with Hugo Vickers (the Trust's Fourth Chairman).

It has occasioned some memorable celebrations and unveilings at key moments in the current reign. And finally, in 2012, it burgeoned into the Jubilee Greenway, a 60 kilometre route through Central London and the suburbs to celebrate the Diamond Jubilee of The Queen, linking a number of key Olympic sites including the main site at Stratford, through which the route passed.

The Jubilee Walkway and the Jubilee Greenway are in a sense gifts to The Queen. As such they are also gifts to the people of London and the many who visit London from all corners of the globe. It celebrates, unites and in some cases defines London. The Jubilee Walkway is a lasting legacy from The Queen's Silver Jubilee in 1977.

The atmosphere surrounding the celebration of the 1977 Silver Jubilee was uncertain since the general public was not especially engaged by it until it was almost upon them. Historically, it has usually taken a lone though distinguished voice to inspire celebrations of this kind to happen. It was the Committee of Merchants and Bankers of London who, in 1809, provided the spark for George III to celebrate his Golden Jubilee the following year, shortly before that Hanoverian monarch fell victim to the long illness which caused the Regency Act of 1811 to be passed and made any idea of celebrating a Diamond Jubilee quite unthinkable. The King died shortly before reaching that significant anniversary, having reigned 59 years and 96 days.

Queen Victoria was in deep mourning at the time that should have marked her Silver Jubilee in 1862, which fell too soon after the death of Prince Albert. On 2 September 1885 the 5th Lord Braye, a Liberal Unionist and Catholic peer, was the inspired figure who promoted the celebration of the Golden Jubilee of 1887 by writing to *The Times*. He noted that the Queen was 'entering upon her 50th year . . . a year of Jubilee.'

The 1887 Jubilee was a family celebration. By

1897 the appetite for a Diamond Jubilee was strong. But Queen Victoria had no wish to entertain a lot of relations from Europe, so she converted it into an Empire celebration. Lady Diana Cooper told me in 1980 that she had sat on the shoulders of her father and watched troops from across the globe march and ride past in their colourful uniforms, and then observed 'the tiny black bundle under a parasol' that was Queen Victoria herself, on her way to St Paul's Cathedral. The 1897 Jubilee led to the creation of many public parks and gardens in London, including Queen's Wood at Highgate and Queen's Park at Kilburn.

In 1934 plans were put forward for the celebration of George V's Silver Jubilee the following year. The King was a little diffident about 'all this fuss and expense about our Jubilee. What will people think of it, in these hard and anxious times?' but he was touched by the spontaneous reception given to him by the British people. This Jubilee and the death of the King soon afterwards in January 1936, resulted in money being raised for a national memorial. The surplus was given as grants towards acquiring

The Palace of Westminster from The Queen's Walk.

sites for playing fields such as King George's Fields in the East End. These playing fields are subject to protective covenants and their gates bear the symbols of lion and unicorn plaques.

All these precedents insured that Buckingham Palace and the Home Office were not going to let The Queen's Silver Jubilee pass unnoticed. Once again the celebrations did not happen by chance and they nearly did not happen at all. The Labour Government with James Callaghan as Prime Minister voted no funds towards the festivities.

Sir Reg Goodwin, Labour Leader of the Greater London Council from 1974, who had worked under Herbert Morrison, realised that the London local authorities would do themselves no credit if they did not celebrate the Jubilee. In 1926 the London County Council had voted £100,000 towards the General Strike, but their successor, the GLC, appeared to be prepared to give nothing to this Jubilee. In the teeth of potential political adversity, Sir James Swaffield, Director-General of the GLC,

The Royal Family on the balcony of Buckingham Palace at the end of the Silver Jubilee celebrations. Lord Mountbatten is standing between The Queen and Princess Anne.

went to see The Queen's Private Secretary to find out what could be done, bearing in mind that there should be 'nothing on the rates', as Sir Reg put it.

This approach resulted in two routes, respectively north and south of the River Thames, for The Queen and The Duke of Edinburgh to be driven along on separate half-days in order to pay formal visits to all the riparian boroughs en route. Additionally a River Progress was arranged with disembarkations at a variety of points and the programme as a whole would provide opportunities for local celebrations to involve a considerable number of Londoners, especially children, as spectators.

Illtyd Harrington, Deputy Leader of the GLC, took a more public stand, anxious that Jubilee celebrations might prove inadequate. He wrote to the *Evening Standard* launching a campaign on 5 August 1975, under the headline: 'Let's plan a Royal Jubilee Festival now!' Harrington had

ambitious plans. His public challenge prompted the Home Secretary, Roy Jenkins, to announce in the House of Commons that the Jubilee would indeed be celebrated in the summer of 1977. He made the point that 'the Government are considering how the occasion might most appropriately be marked in compliance with The Queen's express wish that

Illtyd Harrington cleaning the South Bank Lion, 1977.

undue expenditure should be avoided.'

These joint exhortations prompted others to rise to the challenge. Amongst those who popped up was Max Nicholson. As noted, he was an extraordinary figure, a distinguished environmentalist and ornithologist. He was author of *The System*, a book which had ruffled feathers in government circles and had been a key figure in the Festival of Britain in 1951. Max later said that Illtyd 'clearly hadn't a clue what was involved in running such a Festival,' but immediately responded to his letter in the *Evening Standard* by writing: 'Your challenging proposals certainly ring a bell with me.' He put forward a plan for a Royal Jubilee Festival in London.

As a result of this, Charles Wintour, Editor of the *Evening Standard*, called a meeting to discuss the ideas and the London Celebrations Committee for The Queen's Silver Jubilee was formed. The team which ran it were an eclectic mixture, representing all the elements that were needed. The Chairman was the Earl of Drogheda, a patrician figure, a Knight of the Garter, who had been Chairman of the *Financial Times* and of the Royal Opera House, Covent Garden. A handsome man who moved easily in royal circles, he was a friend and neighbour of the Queen Mother's, living as he did at Englefield Green; he was adept at getting his own way. He could be precise, difficult, mercurial, but he possessed an abundance of charm. When running Covent Garden, he defined his philosophy: 'When things go well, I want to take the credit. When things go wrong, I want to know who to blame.' He was married to a beautiful wife, Joan Carr, a talented pianist with a mysterious and complicated early life.

Their marriage survived a two-year wartime separation during which she was in America. When he went to meet her, he found that a young Frenchman called Roget had fallen madly in love with her. Roget appeared at their hotel in Washington and told Lord Drogheda he must hand Joan over to him. When informed that this was out of the question, the Frenchman drew a knife from his pocket and stabbed himself in the chest. As Lord Drogheda wrote: 'I had never previously, nor have subsequently, had to contend with such melodramatic behaviour.' The incident was not reported in the press. The young man died not long afterwards. Lord Drogheda proved the ideal man for the formal occasions, adding considerable presence to all events he attended.

Jeffrey Sterling, Chairman of Town & City Properties, became Deputy Chairman and Treasurer. His background was very different. He came from the East End, had been a talented violinist as a child, but realised that this would not support him. He went into property and was to rise to be Chairman of P & O. He had considerable vision. When setting up his Committee, he made sure he had a powerful contact in every area of London life, from civic to sport, from culture to the environment. If there was ever a hitch, he knew whom to call. In this there was something of the Mafioso – he would surely not be offended at being likened to Bob Hoskins in the film, *The Long Good Friday*.

Without Jeffrey Sterling, there would have been no London Celebrations Committee and but meagre celebrations in both 1977 and 2002. He raised the money to make it all possible. He has been a consistent supporter of the Jubilee Walkway ever since 1977. He did not always do things by charm. He could be aggressive, but he was effective. When Huggins failed to deliver the flags, he put him on speakerphone and shouted at him down the line. I sat at Jeffrey's side, feeding him with verbal ammunition. You could hear the tremor in Huggins's voice as he formulated his feeble excuses.

On 15 January 1976, a little before this, Patrick Moberly, then in the Personnel Policy Department at the Foreign Office, confirmed that Lord Drogheda's Committee was 'to co-ordinate the various *unofficial* events which will take place in London,' and that 'Lord Drogheda has been given a free hand in selecting people to serve on the Committee.' The Home Office had confirmed that the Home Secretary would soon be giving a statement in the House of Commons 'welcoming its formation'. On 29 January Roy Jenkins duly declared he was pleased to learn of the establishment of this Committee and said: 'No doubt Lord Drogheda and his colleagues will wish to maintain close contacts with the Chairman of the Arts and Sports Council with a view to achieving a co-ordinated programme of activities.'

Sir Paul Wright hoisting the Jubilee flag on 4 Carlton Gardens, 1977.

small fry in those days to merit the charm he was capable of deploying. He fell ill while all the work was being done, mysteriously recovering just in time to enjoy the celebrations. He had claimed to be very ill indeed but, as it turned out, he lived to be 90, finally dying in 2005. Small things are telling. He used to try to put his parking tickets down against the London Celebrations Committee. (They did not pay them). Nevertheless he had many friends and acquaintances. Something of his character can be gleaned from the lines he wrote on leaving the Foreign Office – *An Ambassador's Farewell*:

Of intrigue and deviousness, never a mention,
Not a word about spies, whether truth or invention.
MI5, MI6, they have never existed.
The KGB bimbos are always resisted.
No lover, no mistress, no blot on the file,
And always the fatuous, meaningless smile.
That is the story they all have to tell.
The final communiqué has to read well.

I am afraid that I too wrote a few lines of doggerel about John Denison when he seemed to stay on rather long at the office once the Jubilee celebrations were over. I suppose it is indicative of the tensions that arise when a disparate group come together for an intense period of activity and achievement:

Cultural Chairman, I am he
But they want me out *quam celerrime*,
Ipso facto, verbatim, per se,
Quoi que l'on dise -
I'm here to stay.

* * * * *

The London Celebrations Committee inspired all the major Jubilee celebrations in London, ranging from opera and the arts, concerts, exhibitions, sporting events, local celebrations in the boroughs, and a number of environmental improvements. Max Nicholson chaired the Environmental Committee, assisted by Sir Misha Black (another Festival of Britain man, who had later founded the DRU – Design Research Unit, and who died during Silver Jubilee Year on 11 October), Neville Labovitch,

Lord Drogheda asked for the services of Sir Paul Wright, Special Representative of the Secretary of State at the Foreign Office. This role earned Sir Paul the sobriquet of 'the Smiler' in certain circles as one of his duties was to greet distinguished overseas visitors at the airport. Because Sir Paul was employed by the Foreign Office, this required the blessing of the Prime Minister, who agreed it would be 'an excellent appointment.' Mr Callaghan stipulated that 'the work will be part-time and that his official duties as Special Representative will continue to take priority if necessary over other engagements.'

Sir Paul Wright became Secretary-General to the Committee. One of his early duties was to hoist the Silver Jubilee flag above 4 Carlton Gardens at a photo opportunity. Chris Green, the London Celebrations Committee's press officer, recalled seeing Sir Paul 'clinging onto the railings for dear life on that final ascent to the very rooftop. None of us had realised that he suffered from severe vertigo.'

A retired ambassador, Wright had been a kind of director of public relations at the time of the Festival of Britain and had worked closely with men such as Max, Sir Huw Wheldon and Sir Hugh Casson. Personally I was never a Paul Wright fan, being too

Michael Middleton, Robert Shaw (the first Chairman) and Neville Labovitch (the second Chairman).

Michael Middleton (Civic Trust), Sir Paul Reilly (Design Council) and Robert Shaw (a Planning Officer of the GLC).

The origin of the Jubilee Walkway can be found in a document prepared by Max Nicholson on 4 March 1976. On 11 March he presented it the London Celebrations Committee as part of his environmental programme:

Silver Jubilee Heritage Walkway or Trail

Proposed to be waymarked with the Silver Jubilee emblem and to run some five miles in all from the newly pedestrianised Leicester Square, by Trafalgar Square, St James's Park and the Houses of Parliament, over Lambeth Bridge and thence along the South Bank to Tower Bridge (with temporary diversions where Thames-side access is still incomplete), ending up at St Katharine's Dock and the Tower of London.
This would include several new GLC works, including the promenade in front of the National Theatre, the new embankment at Blackfriars/Bankside and the site now used as a car park by Tower Bridge/Potters Fields. It is hoped to clear the Dome of Discovery site next to County Hall by demolishing the huts near the railway and moving the car park to that area, thus providing a first-class venue for events, and an opportunity to plant a Jubilee Grove of trees.

The London Celebrations Committee welcomed the project and by June 1976 Nicholson was confident that there would be something for The Queen to open when she came to the Shell Building on 9 June 1977 to witness a fabulous firework display over the Thames.

At the same time Max defined what a walkway was and what he planned for this one. As early as 1617 it was applied to 'a course or circuit which may be chosen for walking' with the added implication that the course should be pre-arranged for that purpose and that the walker would be safeguarded from disturbance by other forms of traffic. This one was designed to do the following:

To revive the paramount role of the Thames itself, as the spine and setting of London.

By means of a linking silver thread to draw together the long divorced worlds of the West End, the South Bank, East London and the City.

To display and relate many old landmarks and new improvements which few visitors or even Londoners would otherwise come to appreciate as a whole, composing the symphony of London.

To demonstrate and explain factually something of the essential nature, the geography and the history of London for students of all ages.

An early map showing the route of the Silver Jubilee Walkway.

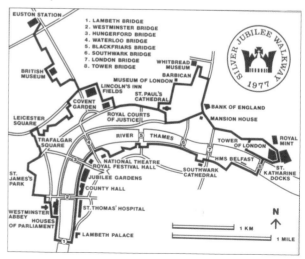

Early designs for markers, later rejected.

To encourage the best way of getting to know London – on foot – and to reassert the full equality of the walker with others moving by other means.

To focus the fast growing interest in conserving and improving London's environment, and to help bring together and stimulate those who share it.

The Silver Jubilee Walkway was the foremost of what Max Nicholson called his 'Seven Thrusts' – a document designed to inspire activity in varying ways at the time of the Jubilee. In the summer of 1977, at a sporting event in Hyde Park, Max told me of his plans, speaking of the Thames as 'the spine of London', seeking to narrow the divide between north and south London, and his other plans – not least to develop 40,000 acres of disused land scattered about the capital. He made it all sound so simple, so sensible and such fun.

Max saw the merits of an urban city trail similar to many such trails he had created in the British countryside in the course of his long career. The Silver Jubilee Walkway was to be an urban trail promoted by the Civic Trust to interpret architectural features and aspects of townscape, passing as it much of it would, through the built environment. Max's aim was to lure people onto the South Bank and past the site of the Festival of Britain. He wanted the Jubilee Walkway to help open up the South Bank of the Thames and this vision was to prove an immeasurable success. He realised that if the route were associated with the Jubilee, then it would fall into place much more easily than otherwise. If you want to build a village hall and you call it the Jubilee Hall, funds tend to be more readily available.

Max also said that someone walking the Jubilee Walkway would have travelled through areas of London noted for entertainment, assembly, ceremonial and open-air activity and past many historic sites. He would have been enticed from the West End onto the South Bank and into the City. Max hoped that 'perhaps he will be subtly changed by what he has absorbed from this fertile heritage.' It was always seen as more than just a route or promenade with the opportunity for trees and other things to enjoy along the way.

It was still a bit of a battle, Max writing that the idea of a city walkway was 'novel and needed both explaining and popularising. I therefore had to hark back to my earliest occupation as a guide-book writer, turning out a 72 page illustrated historical guide entitled The Silver Jubilee Walkway together with a folder map to show the way along it.' This was the guidebook, financed by the Civic Trust and eventually distributed by W.H. Smith Distributors.

Max was generally pleased with the way things progressed, and in particular in how the bureaucrats were supporting the Jubilee, and, as he put in a

Lord Ponsonby of Shulbrede with the Earl of Drogheda, 1977.

letter, 'their participation in promoting the Jubilee has been most encouraging and highly appreciated, not least by those who often say rude things about them such as, yours faithfully, Max Nicholson.'

The Environmental Committee based itself at 26-28 Old Queen Street, made available to them by the GLC. By 2 July 1976 Sir Paul Wright confirmed that The Queen 'had expressed her interest in, and approval of, the Silver Jubilee Walkway scheme.' Matters moved quickly. By September a survey had been undertaken, the signing was designed, plans were underway to demolish old warehouses near Southwark Cathedral opening it to a Thames view, improvements were being undertaken at Tower Hill, and the City Corporation was considering extending the Walkway to St Paul's Cathedral.

By October the Walkway had been guaranteed a grant of £25,000 from the GLC. Valuable support also came from Robert Shaw, Planning Officer of the GLC and James Kennedy, Chief Officer of GLC Parks Department. The GLC helped surreptitiously through planning budgets and so forth. Not everything ran smoothly, the way-markers proved a problem and there were some 'minor but tiresome' difficulties in the Parliament Square and Millbank area.

On 16 May South Bank Jubilee Gardens were handed over to the GLC by the London Celebrations

The demolition of some old warehouses to allow a view of Southwark Cathedral from the river was one of the Trust's first successes.

The Queen opening the Jubilee Walkway at the South Bank Lion, 9 June 1977, watched by Lord Drogheda.

Committee in a topping-out ceremony and Lord Drogheda presented Lord Ponsonby of Shulbrede with a scroll.

The Queen was pleased that there would be a permanent legacy of her Jubilee and one that could be enjoyed by the many who might walk it in the years to come. It goes without saying that The Queen much appreciates gifts which can also be of wide public benefit.

It was an exceptionally wet night when The Queen opened the Silver Jubilee Walkway on 9 June. Earlier in the day there had been a River Progress up the Thames. In the evening the Royal Family came to the 24th floor of the Shell Building to watch a spectacular fireworks display. The Queen and The Duke of Edinburgh arrived at the GLC

building for a reception. They were due to exit via an Embankment level door. This was locked and there was a moment of panic when no one could find the key but it turned up just in time for them to make a dignified exit and walk to the steps of Westminster Bridge. There were a great number of accredited photographers present, but Chris Green recalled 'having to physically hold back a couple of over-enthusiastic red-top photographers,' his first experience of 'the media gone mad.'

There The Queen formally opened the Walkway by unveiling a plaque on the plinth of the South Bank Lion which stands on the south-west corner of the bridge. This lion was originally made in 1837 and was one of a pair that stood on the Red Lion Brewery, both painted red in those days. The brewery was demolished in 1949, by which time the lion been noticed by George VI, who took a liking to him. One of the lions was sent to Twickenham Stadium,

24

where, painted gold, he guards the Rowland Hill Memorial Gate. The other lion was first moved to Waterloo Station, but following extension work there, he was moved to his present site. He had been saved from a terrible fate by the direct intervention of the King. The panel depicting the opening of the Walkway can still be seen on the plinth to this day.

The Queen then walked a small part of the Walkway, past the GLC's County Hall and unveiled a panel to open the newly restored Jubilee Gardens. Lord Drogheda recalled:

> The walk was a few hundred yards long, passing through a new Jubilee garden financed with money raised by Jeffrey Sterling from the Hayward Foundation, with contributions also from Shell and the GLC. I walked slightly behind the Queen, and I felt the full force of the cheering. The noise was deafening, and in a way quite alarming; but all the time the Queen smiled dazzlingly, and I could observe at first hand what was aptly described to me by a member of her entourage [Sir Martin Charteris] as her love affair with the British people.

The Queen entered the Shell Building for dinner, watched the fireworks, neither the display nor the enthusiasm of the crowds dampened by the rain of the evening. Of those watching with her, one was James Callaghan, the Prime Minister. Charles Wintour recalled standing next to him. 'Just what the country needed!' declared the Prime Minister. Wintour reminded him gently that the nation had paid nothing towards it. 'I don't mind how much it

The Queen opening Jubilee Gardens a few moments later.

cost,' continued the Prime Minister, 'it is just what was needed' – easy words for a politician who had contributed nothing.

Those of us lucky enough to be in the Shell Building that evening had the strange experience of seeing the fireworks without hearing them. Chris Green recalled: 'They burst magnificently in front of us at eye level with the dullest of cracking sounds because of the double glazing – all a little surreal.' The Queen then returned to Buckingham Palace by carriage and appeared on the balcony of Buckingham Palace, cheered by a huge and amiable crowd.

The Story of the Jubilee Walkway Trust

At the end of Jubilee year, when the celebrations were over, the London Celebrations Committee was wound up. There was some money left over. This was destined for the Silver Jubilee Trust (which had succeeded King George's Jubilee Trust, and was run in 1977 by The Prince of Wales, funds helping to create the Prince's Trust). Before that, Jeffrey Sterling, the Treasurer, handed over some funds to the Walkway to assist in its completion and development.

The question arose as to how this should be administered. Sir James Swaffield was anxious that the Walkway should 'avoid political controversy and be independent of GLC control.' Sir James explained: 'Control would lie with the Trustees (subject to the Charity Commission) and be liable to

modification, extension or conclusion as whatever they, by simple majority, might decide.'

Therefore, early in the following year, on 23 February 1978, the Silver Jubilee Walkway Trust met in Room 146 of The County Hall, and, following their discussions, Memorandum and Articles of Association were produced and signed on 12 October that year. On 6 February 1979 the Trust was incorporated under the Companies Act 1948 to 1976 and registered as a charity on 11 April.

The Trust sought a royal Patron. The ideal choice was The Duke of Gloucester. He was the younger son of Prince Henry, Duke of Gloucester and a first cousin of The Queen. As a young man he had studied architecture and had hoped to lead a relatively Bohemian life practising architecture and living on the Isle of Dogs. But his elder brother, Prince William, was killed in a flying accident in

Early Trustees and others at County Hall. Sir James Swaffield (third Chairman), front row right.

St Katharine Docks from the River Thames.

1972, after which he moved to Kensington Palace, took on royal duties and ran the family estate at Barnwell Manor. The Duke had always taken a keen interest in London, its buildings and development. He had produced a book of photographs of the city – *The Face of London* – in 1973. He accepted the Trust's invitation and has been a hugely supportive Patron of the Trust, attending fundraising lunches, holding meetings, unveiling panels and advising officials of the Trust privately. Over the years the Trust was also greatly supported by the Duke's three successive Private Secretaries, Sir Simon Bland, Major Nicholas Barne and Alistair Wood.

The objects of the Trust were defined as to maintain, repair, promote, preserve, protect, improve and (if necessary) extend the Walkway and adjoining features; also, interestingly, to establish 'similar public walkways in any part of Britain and Northern Ireland.' The latter has not happened, but, after these many years, there are plans to expand in that direction. All kinds of legal provisos were put in place and 14 Trustees appointed, of whom only one now serves – Kate Trevelyan.

Robert Shaw was the Chairman and the others were George Chandler, Peter Drew, Robert Green (honorary Treasurer), David Hamilton (honorary Secretary), Neville Labovitch, George Mann, Michael Middleton, Anthony Prendergast, Lord Reilly, Lord Ponsonby of Shulbrede, David Senior and Kate Trevelyan. John Kaye joined the original team that day. A full list of Trustees is given in Appendix 2.

The Trust's goals were to make the existing route more usable, to extend it where possible and to encourage people to walk in London. In order to do this, the Trust needed to rely on the support of the local authorities for the Boroughs through which the Walkway passed, and also on outside sponsorship. In the early days this usually came from companies with premises close to the Walkway. Their major initiative was to improve and promote the South Bank, open a riparian route along the Thames, and integrate the South Bank into Central London, thus stimulating a variety of improvements.

An early plan was to complete the circuit of the Walkway via Covent Garden and back to Leicester Square. Another was to create a loop to take in St Katharine Docks. In due course 385 markers were

ABOVE A gold marker.

LEFT A gold marker in the Mall; a silver marker on the South Bank.

fixed into the ground throughout the Walkway to mark the route, especially where it changed direction. These were finally cast in high grade aluminium by the long established firm of Butler Jones (Nameplates) Ltd of Bognor Regis. These markers and the bronze plaque unveiled by The Duke of Gloucester in Chancery Lane were paid for by the London Celebrations Committee.

* * * * *

The Northern arm of the Walkway, a three-mile extension, was launched on 14 July 1978 when The Duke of Gloucester unveiled a plaque on a pillar outside the Public Record Office in Chancery Lane (later taken over by King's College, London) at a ceremony attended by the Lord Mayors of London and Westminster, the Mayor of Camden and the Chairman of the GLC. In a letter to Lord Drogheda, Max Nicholson described this as 'the last public event of the Jubilee.' He continued: 'The opening ceremony went off smoothly in so much better weather than The Queen had at the South Bank Lion last year, and the redesigned (for the fourth time!) pavement markers seem to be the final answer

The Duke of Gloucester with Robert Shaw opening the new Walkway loop through the City of London in Chancery Lane on 14 July 1978.

Rt Hon Michael Heseltine after unveiling his panel at Hay's Wharf in June 1991. HMS *Belfast* and Tower Bridge are in the background.

in terms of elegance and durability.'

There was also a last minute mile long extension from St Paul's Cathedral to the Museum of London and the headquarters of Whitbread's Brewery, mapped out with the help of one of the Trustees, George Chandler, former City of London Architect.

In order to promote all this, Brian Taylor of the Inner London Education Authority's Television Centre, made a film about the Walkway which he showed to schools in Inner London, to increase awareness of this new feature of the Capital city. 30,000 Walkway maps were produced and 10,000 soon sold.

In 1979 the Bloomsbury Spur of the Walkway was incorporated and on 3 October The Duke of Gloucester unveiled a plaque at Euston Station with some stirring speeches both at the unveiling and also at the subsequent lunch hosted by British Rail. This spur of the Walkway has since been continued to form a loop.

Assembly markers (the Gothic crown on a pole) were placed in Leicester Square, Parliament Square, on the South Bank, and by Southwark Cathedral. Diagrammatic maps were attached to these. Only two now survive, the one on the South Bank near Jubilee Gardens and the one in Parliament Square (now dedicated to the memory of Neville Labovitch).

Panoramic panels, then described as 'visual indicators', were first introduced in 1980, not only

on the Walkway itself, but also on the Embankment and on many of London's bridges to identify the buildings along the way. Their designer was a man with a fascinatingly diverse life – David Seigle-Morris (1925-2005), of Capital Design, one of the interesting characters who helped make the Trust such a success. As a young man he had driven in numerous car rallies, taking part in the Monte Carlo

The assembly marker by Jubilee Gardens.

Rally of 1958 in an MG Magnette. Ford signed him for the 1963 season and he continued rallying until 1966. In 1968 he took part in the *Daily Express* London to Sydney Marathon and in 1970 was on the organizing team of the 1970 London to Mexico World Cup Rally.

As a professional architect he had even designed his own house at Gravesend, Kent, when still at architectural college. He became Head of Furniture and Design at the LCC (later GLC) and House Architect for the Royal Festival Hall and the Queen Elizabeth Hall, a post he held until the GLC was dissolved in 1986. He also ran a Gulf garage in Sydenham. Amongst his many other interests he played classical and jazz on the piano and was a talented painter. One of his colleagues was eventually less appreciated. When Robert Shaw criticised some careless errors on one of the panels and suggested that whoever was responsible might like to contribute towards correcting these, the two parted company, the designer less than amicably.

Panoramic panels were a new concept for the Walkway, a means of assisting those using the Walkway to identify the various buildings and landmarks along the way. Arguably this is a job that should have been done by the London Tourist Board or some similar body, but it was soon to become an important feature of the work of the Walkway Trust. They have also provided the Trust with the opportunity to invite many famous and distinguished figures to unveil them.

Over the years panels have been unveiled by Her Majesty The Queen and HRH The Duke of Edinburgh, HRH The Prince of Wales, HRH The Countess of Wessex, HRH The Duke of Gloucester, and President Nelson Mandela (during his State Visit to Britain in 1996). In 1980 the first two were unveiled – one at Lambeth Palace and another in Parliament Square, both in October. A full list of Panoramic Panels appears in Appendix 3.

By 1981 markers had been provided for the first 5½ km of the Walkway, which now extended some 8½ km in all. A loop had been added to the north side of the Walkway from the Mansion House via the Barbican (spanning the lake there) to St Paul's Cathedral. By then 400 pavement markers were

Robert Shaw receiving the Europa Nostra Award from Sir Ashley Bramall and Lord Duncan-Sandys in 1982.

in the ground. Robert Shaw became aware of the proposed development of the Hay's Wharf area between London Bridge and Tower Bridge, a case where the creation of the riparian route became a condition of the planning permission grant. The developers were happy to comply.

Joyce Bellamy, then working in the Department for Recreation and Arts at the GLC, and writing on behalf of the Assistant Director, Planning, made her first appearance on a Walkway matter in March 1982, discussing how the GLC could help the Walkway with its ongoing projects and urging the GLC to support the Trust. She was especially keen that financial support should be given to the design of more panoramic panels. She stressed that the new panels were a great success and that they had proved to be 'immensely attractive and informative to visitors, who can usually be seen crowding around them' – a feature that continues to this day.

Robert Shaw was keen to add two or three panels a year and found sponsors for panels at the Royal Exchange, Trafalgar Square (north side), Waterloo Place and Trafalgar Square (south west). Joyce recommended £5,000 from the GLC. She attended a meeting of the Trust on 12 May. Her next proposal was to get the Walkway along the river fronting the IBM development. There was a lot of discussion and many a memo passed before the precise route was agreed.

Presently the GLC's design work for the Walkway secured an Europa Nostra Award. Sir Ashley Bramall, then Chairman of the Greater London Council, hosted a reception at which the Award was presented to the GLC 'on account of the Silver Jubilee Walkway'. Lord Duncan-Sandys, President of Europa Nostra, and Sir Ashley presented the award to Robert Shaw, who accepted it on behalf of the Trust. Lord Duncan-Sandys described the Walkway as 'an imaginative project which will bring interest and enjoyment to countless people of all ages across the world.' From then on Joyce Bellamy became a regular attendee of the Trust's meetings.

The Westminster Bridge underpass was first proposed in February 1983, and the point was made that it formed 'a key section of the Silver Jubilee Walkway'. This was an important development. Until the underpass was built, the Walkway ran along Albert Embankment from Lambeth Palace to Westminster Bridge. It was then necessary to climb the steps and cross over the bridge before rejoining the route at County Hall. The underpass united the two sections, greatly improving the riverside route, avoiding the dangers of having to battle with traffic on Westminster Bridge itself, and with obvious

London Bridge and St Paul's Cathedral from the South Bank.

benefits for disabled and elderly people.

Joyce Bellamy began to press Robert Shaw into adding new features to the map and adopting the new theme of the location of gardens as resting, assembly and picnic points along the route of the Walkway to develop it from being a route into something wider. This theme Joyce promoted with vigour for the next 28 years.

IBM's new London Marketing Centre opened with a view of an excellent stretch of the river. They recalled that this had been marshland, reclaimed by the Black Prince in the 14th century and later to become the mooring place for Royal Barges in the days of the Tudors. Sir Christopher Wren had made his home there, opposite the site of his great masterpiece, St Paul's Cathedral. This view was now placed at the disposal of all Londoners, with a wonderful riverside promenade, with lampposts and railings. In those days, St Paul's Cathedral still dominated the London skyline, but that alas was soon to change.

Sir James Swaffield was about to retire as

Director-General of the GLC. Having taken such a strong interest in the Trust, to the point that he was virtually its father figure, the Trustees were keen that he should formally join their number. He did so in December 1983.

During the next few years the Walkway inched its way along the South Bank. It was already possible to walk from Blackfriars Bridge to Bankside Power Station. Many used it to get to work, arriving at Waterloo Station and then walking to their offices. Robert Shaw monitored plans for Hay's Wharf and there were signs that the Walkway would lead all the way to Tower Bridge alongside the river.

1985 proved to be a dramatic year. For two years Margaret Thatcher's Government had been in conflict with Ken Livingstone at the GLC, and the Local Government Act 1985 was passed, meaning that the GLC would be closed down on 31 March 1986. The implications for the Walkway were potentially grave.

* * * * *

A more serious tragedy involved David Hamilton, a founder Trustee, who was last seen alive on 18 November 1985. He had been present at a lunch at County Hall on 26 April at which The Duke of Gloucester, Ken Livingstone and a number of figures related to the Walkway were present. But after November he was never seen again. To read the Trust's bland minutes, it is clear that he was still considered to be the Honorary Secretary until March 1986.

At a meeting of the Executive Committee on 17 December 1985 Robert Shaw explained that 'David Hamilton had been taken ill and was likely to be away for some time. He agreed to write to him conveying the good wishes of the Trustees for a speedy recovery.' Invitations to a further lunch at County Hall on 19 February 1986 were sent out with Hamilton's name as RSVP. But since he was not around, Miss Margaret Beckett's telephone number was given for the replies.

The work of the Trust had to go on and for the now understandable reason that he was dead, Hamilton failed to appear at a Jubilee Walkway meeting at County Hall. Joyce Bellamy was asked to go along the corridor to take the minutes. On 26 March 1986 Robert Shaw, who had been working closely with Joyce over Trust matters since 1982, wrote to her, 'delighted that you have been able to agree to take on the mantle of Honorary Secretary in place of David Hamilton.' The Annual Report for 1985-1986 recorded that Hamilton had 'had to withdraw as Honorary Secretary due to ill health.' Joyce was confirmed as Honorary Secretary at the Executive Committee meeting on 20 May.

One of Joyce's first duties was to get the Trust out of what Robert Shaw called 'a pickle' with Companies House, since no returns had been submitted on behalf of the Trust for 1980, 1981 or 1982, David Hamilton having neglected to file these.

It was not until considerably later that Hamilton's fate became known. He lived in an elegant house at 164 Brixton Road, where he took in a gay lover called Kingsley Rotardier. After Hamilton disappeared, Rotardier told a neighbour that his friend had been diagnosed with AIDS and had discreetly retired to a clinic in Hanover in Germany. The neighbour was suspicious and when, some weeks later, he observed credit card statements arriving addressed to Hamilton, he went to the police.

Rotardier was questioned and a number of suspicious circumstances convinced Detective Inspector John Scullion that Hamilton had been murdered. But he had no proof, so could only charge Rotardier with credit card fraud.

Rotardier had been full of stories. He had arranged for forged postcards to be sent to Hamilton's brother and cleaning lady from as far away as Malaysia. Scullion investigated and found that no Hamilton had travelled to an AIDS clinic in Paris or Hanover or taken a flight to Malaysia. A lot of other information proved to be contradictory, including a letter to the GLC purporting to come from Hamilton in which he resigned due to serious illness. Since the GLC was being abolished, this meant he seemed to be surrendering six months of salary (£17,000) and a pension of £6,000 a year.

In December 1986 Rotardier pleaded guilty to six charges of fraud relating to Hamilton's credit cards. Sentencing was deferred until 5 January 1987, on which day he was given a 9 month suspended prison sentence. He emerged from court at which point Scullion arrested him on suspicion of murder.

Police investigations produced further inconsistencies and finally an inspection of transactions on Hamilton's credit cards showed that Rotardier had gone to a catering supply company in Clapham and purchased a butcher's meat cleaver and a butcher's bone saw. Though the body was never found, the conclusion was that he had been murdered, cut up in the bath and incinerated under darkness in the garden. Rotardier was jailed for life, with a recommendation that he serve 20 years.

It was not until 10 June 1987 that a Memorial Service for David Napier Hamilton was held in Southwark Cathedral, at which his friend, Illtyd Harrington, now also a Trustee, gave the address. He said:

> His impeccable dress and old-fashioned good manners were odd compared to our rough ways, but his souped-up bangers and his delight in rebuilding a Bentley confounded those who saw him as an elegant intellectual. He would have held his own amongst the skilled workmen in the toolroom at Fords of Dagenham, with a little demotic help from myself. The son of an inventor, he had a built-in genetic advantage and enormous practical gifts – he was a brilliant photographer – and to be asked to his table was to enjoy good food and wine and stimulating, even passionate, conversation. He gathered a cabinet of talents all around him.

Harrington spoke of Hamilton's life in Ethiopia and his service with the founder of the SAS, Colonel David Stirling, in Rhodesia. He had been Private Secretary to the Governor of the West Indies, Headmaster and Commanding Officer of Massawa College and earned a D. Phil at Oxford. The Prime Minister of Dominica sent a message: 'We are saddened by his passing and grieved at the manner of his death. He was such a gentle man that we find it difficult to associate violence with him.' Illtyd concluded:

> David has bequeathed us a long and poignant sadness which he would be the first to urge us to allow to pass. He was no plaster saint. His vulnerability, perhaps at times his gullibility worried his friends but, somehow, we felt he would shine through.

Robert Shaw, Illtyd Harrington and David Hamilton.

Joyce Bellamy meeting The Queen outside Buckingham Palace, February 2012.

* * * * *

Following the abolition of the GLC in 1986, the Trust's work was overseen by the London Residuary Body which mopped up outstanding GLC commitments. This included tree planting along the South Bank, the trees requiring carefully constructed tree pits to prevent the soil seeping away. After that London lacked a strategic planning office, and not until the Greater London Authority and Transport for London were formed in 2000, did cohesion return.

Lord Birkett, a stalwart supporter of the Trust, was one who expressed considerable concern as to how the abolition of the GLC would affect the

Trust. On 16 January he wrote to William H. Stubbs, Education Officer of the Inner London Education Authority, explaining that the GLC had helped with 'expertise and ceremonial', but, 'most importantly the architects have always provided the services of planning the Walkway and designing its plaques & indicators [Panoramic Panels]. My own department [the Department for Recreation and the Arts] isn't the "lead" in this matter but we have always tried to be helpful and Joyce Bellamy from our small strategy group has been a tireless enthusiast.'

He suggested that the architects coming over from the ILEA should continue their services to the Walkway. By this method he hoped to prevent the Trust from folding. A while later Stubbs replied that the architects coming over from the ILEA would like to help but on 'a cost-recoverable basis'. He hoped that would be a satisfactory solution. The Trust rejected this offer in favour of direct contact with a designer of their own choosing.

Joyce Bellamy, Illtyd Harrington and William Crossley became Trustees that year. From 1982 onwards Joyce had performed a double act with Robert Shaw when planning requests came in on the South Bank. He was an expert on planning and she on parks: 'We were like Laurel and Hardy.' Gradually the route opened along the South Bank, eventually crystallising as The Queen's Walk. As Sir James Swaffield wrote, the Walkway Trust might have been wound up like the London Celebrations Committee, 'but the enthusiasm of the initial Trustees led by Robert Shaw and Joyce Bellamy, was sustained by Neville [Labovitch] and others and led to its continued existence and prosperity.'

In 1987 the Trust approached its tenth anniversary. There was a move to change the name from 'Silver Jubilee Walkway' to 'The London Walkway'. The argument put forward was that it was time to expand:

The 'Silver Jubilee' tag is a valuable asset, because of its 'Royal' associations. But informal research suggests it is a two-edged sword: many people believe that the route-markers are merely a relic of the 1977 Silver Jubilee celebrations, and that the Walkway has in some ways become dated. There is widespread awareness of the Walkway, but it is no longer top of mind.

Yet, since 1977, the Walkway has been extended and the number of route-markers and indicator plaques greatly increased. The Walkway is ripe for further promotion as '*The* way to discover London – at your own pace'.

This plan was prepared for the Trust by a team of public relations consultants. These figures so often peddle bad advice in beautifully presented documents with little understanding of the ethos of the business. They then send an exorbitant bill. Their plan proposed the undertaking of various promotions and a new map, there remaining only 3,000 of the original 30,000 maps from 1979 left on sale. The scheme would cost £46,012. Fortunately it was not adopted.

Joyce Bellamy wondered if the idea to drop the 'Silver Jubilee' part of the Walkway owed something to a Republican element in certain circles. Certainly the Walkway occasionally encountered hostility in some boroughs and political units on account of its royal connection. She noted that sometimes Walkway maps were thrown away, people judging them relics of the Silver Jubilee.

In 1988 the tenth anniversary of the Trust arrived and was considered no mean achievement. The Walkway now extended along the Thames as far as Blackfriars Bridge. The Riverside Walk at Coin Street was nearing completion. In January Michael Middleton put forward some ideas for celebration, one of them being 'HM to attend a tenth anniversary event/function'.

The Chairman invited The Queen to visit the Walkway to open the latest stretch. The Queen's Assistant Private Secretary, Robert Fellowes, was keenly supportive and it was agreed that The Queen and The Duke of Edinburgh would visit the Walkway on the afternoon of 7 December. A special leaflet was created to commemorate the occasion. On that day The Queen unveiled a rondel made of granite at the Coin Street riverfront development (the development of which had caused numerous discussions in the Trust). They then walked some of the Walkway, with workers from neighbouring offices coming out to see them pass on their way to a reception at Royal Festival Hall. Before she left The Queen switched on

the lights of a huge Christmas tree outside Festival Hall. This was the most significant walk she has ever taken along the Walkway.

Distinguished guests came out in force, including Robert Runcie, Archbishop of Canterbury, the Lord Mayors of London and Westminster, Lord Drogheda (who died a year later in December 1989), Norman Tebbit and his wife, and Sir Godfrey Taylor, Chairman of the London Residuary Body.

Afterwards Robert Fellowes wrote to Robert Shaw to express The Queen's thanks for 'an unusual and most enjoyable afternoon' adding 'Much has changed in the eleven years since Jubilee Year and it is quite possible that the concept of the Walkway might have been lost had it not been for your tenacity and enthusiasm for the project. Her Majesty hopes that you will make your colleagues aware of just how much she values their selfless efforts to ensure that this twelve mile pathway through London was properly complete.'

The Queen unveiling the Coin Street Rondel on 7 December 1988.

During these years London was forever changing. Plans were announced to change County Hall into a hotel and apartments but without altering the face of the riverside building. Nameplates were needed for The Queen's Walk, new panels were planned, damaged panels were identified for repair. With the route now more or less complete, there was the chance to enhance it by encouraging the planting of gardens adjacent to the Walkway. Jubilee Gardens was under threat due to the Jubilee underground extension being constructed below it. This was an ongoing issue and by the time of the Diamond Jubilee in 2012 these gardens were beautifully restored.

After numerous failed attempts, sponsorship was finally obtained to produce 100,000 new maps of the Walkway, the brewers, Whitbread's and Charrington's, sharing the costs. This was

Political unveilings in Parliament Square. ABOVE Lord Tebbit on 7 October 1980. BELOW Viscount Tonypandy on 27 May 1992.

service, stating: 'He had opponents, but no enemies . . . He was urbane, he appeared to be relaxed, even casual. And yet he was wily and determined when it mattered.' At the end of the year Lady Ponsonby agreed to become a Trustee in her husband's place. In *the Independent* Terence Conran described Lord Reilly as 'a great Design Ambassador for this country.'

When Norman Tebbit unveiled a replacement panel in Parliament Square, he found himself surrounded by the media, the event occurring on 26 November 1990, shortly after the resignation of Margaret Thatcher as Prime Minister after 11 years in office and in the middle of the contest for a new leader for the Conservative Party.

In 1991 Robert Shaw advised on a Walkway in Bombay and another in Lowestoft, the latter at the request of Waveney Borough Council. On 29 January 1992 The Duke of Gloucester lunched with the Trustees at the Headquarters of Mobil Europe, as guests of William Crossley, a great number of the Trust's particular supporters being present.

On 4 June The Queen paid her third visit to the Walkway, coming to Leicester Square to celebrate its reopening after it had been largely pedestrianised. First she unveiled the 20th plaque, and then switched on the London Electricity underground substation beneath it. Since Leicester Square was the symbolic starting point of the Walkway, it had particular importance. Combined with this were the 50 new bronze Commonwealth plaques representing the countries of the Commonwealth, including Namibia, the latest to join. These were placed in their respective geographical positions, with distances marked – and duly checked by the Royal Geographical Society. The Queen met representatives of the Commonwealth Youth Exchange Council and children from Westminster. Afterwards there was a reception in the foyer of the Odeon Cinema, hosted by Westminster City Council.

On 27 January 1993 a new Walkway map was launched at a reception on the 23rd floor of the Shell Centre, attended by The Duke of Gloucester. During these years the Duke frequently assisted the Trust by attending lunches for fundraisers and other distinguished figures.

finally launched at a reception on board the TS *Queen Mary*, a former pleasure steamer on the Clyde in April 1990. The occasion was introduced by Lord Palumbo in the presence of the Lord Mayor of Westminster, many London Mayors and distinguished guests.

In 1990 the Trust lost two of the original Trustees, Lord Ponsonby of Shulbrede in June and Lord Reilly in October. Neil Kinnock spoke at Tom Ponsonby's

The Prince of Wales unveiling the panoramic panel on Tower Bridge on 30 June 1994.

From time to time the Walkway Trust engaged with schools. This year it was arranged that London schools would take part in the Westminster Schools' Art Competition to be judged by Sir Hugh Casson, the idea being to promote interest along the Walkway amongst youngsters. Unfortunately only four schools entered and the proposed exhibition had to be cancelled. This was one of the attempts made by the Trust to heighten awareness and amongst the less successful of its endeavours.

More panels were unveiled. Robert Shaw tried to persuade The Queen Mother to unveil one on Tower Bridge, but she declined. The Prince of Wales agreed to unveil it on 30 June, as part of the centenary celebrations of Tower Bridge. This was a major civic ceremony, with toastmasters, mayors, the Lord Mayor of London, the Remembrancer and many other distinguished figures. It took place 100 years to the day since the then Prince and Princess of Wales (later King Edward VII and Queen Alexandra) had opened Tower Bridge after eight years of construction. At 11.32 Robert Shaw and Michael

Tower Bridge.

Foster, Chairman of Courage (who sponsored the panel) stood opposite The Prince of Wales, the Lord Mayor and Lady Mayoress. Robert Shaw made a short speech inviting the Prince to unveil the panel. The Prince then departed to HM Yacht *Britannia* and the guests enjoyed a luncheon of Orkney Lobster and Fillet of Beef Richelieu in Guildhall.

At this time the Thames Path was created. Joyce Bellamy pointed out that The Queen's Walk was already in place and the then Countryside Commission were able to take advantage of this to adopt the route as part of the Thames Path National Trail, the Trail being opened in 1996.

By November 1994 the new 254metre length of Walkway was ready after six months' work, alongside the river at London Bridge City. This last stretch marked the completion of The Queen's Walk, and seemingly marked the final completion of the entire Silver Jubilee Walkway from Lambeth Palace to Tower Bridge.

Inevitably, questions arose at Trust meetings as to what it should do next, how far the Walkway should expand and whether there were dangers in taking on too much, given the way it was run. In September 1994 Michael Middleton presented a paper with a plan. He noted that following The Queen's visit in November, 'the original purposes of the Walkway Trust could be said to be completed.' He appreciated that there would be the ongoing need to maintain the Walkway and that probably new panels would suggest themselves occasionally, but it was time to contemplate the future. He wondered how the Walkway could be exploited:

> A range of possible events might be considered, for example: a great torchlight procession, perhaps on Midsummer's Night or New Year's Eve. This could be organised to cover half a dozen different sectors, with local schools, youth and community groups participating, each sector 'handing over' to the next in sequence, or converging upon one point for a climactic conclusion (a firework Display?). Alternatively it might be combined with a great sequential firework display, combined with river pageant, stretching from Lambeth Palace to the Tower so that people would line the length of the Walkway on both sides of the River.

Michael Middleton encouraged the idea of a film or video for use in schools, libraries, or the British Council, to be placed in hotels and aired on national television. He thought every panoramic panel should be accompanied by a nearby map dispenser.

He proposed ideas for the extension of the Walkway eastwards into the East End or westwards into Chelsea. He advanced the idea that the Trustees should now turn their attention to playing 'a more active part in the planning and quality of all riparian development and change.' Michael conceded that Trustees might not wish to explore any of this, but if they did, 'there could be no better moment to announce its plans for the future than when The Queen's visit marks the completion of the original Walkway concept.'

As we shall see, some of these ideas did come about, but most did not. Meanwhile the highlight of the year and one of the most significant and important landmarks in the history of the Walkway occurred on 10 November, when The Queen attended a ceremony to mark the completion of this final section.

The Queen arrived with The Duke of Edinburgh in the Royal Barge, docking at London Bridge City Pier, near Hay's Galleria in Tooley Street. She was received by The Duke of Gloucester at 2.45 pm. Also present were Field Marshal Lord Bramall (Lord Lieutenant for the County of London), the Mayor of Southwark, the Secretary-General of the Commonwealth Secretariat, the Ambassador of Kuwait, the President of the Kuwait Investment Office the Managing Director of St Martin's Property Group (developers who had worked so well with the Trust), and of course Robert Shaw, the Walkway's Chairman.

The Lord and Lady Mayoress of Westminster and other London Mayors were presented along with officers of the Trust. Robert Shaw invited Her Majesty to unveil a panoramic panel and a plaque to commemorate the occasion. He made a short speech to which, after a fanfare from the Trumpeters of the Household Cavalry, The Queen replied, saying that she could not promise to walk the whole Walkway herself, but much welcomed its completion. The occasion was followed by a reception.

It was a proud day for the Trust but also one

of poignant sadness. Robert Shaw had worked tirelessly to secure the completion of the Walkway. It was obvious to those who knew him well that he was an extremely ill man. He arrived in a wheelchair but rose from it to greet and thank The Queen. On account of the gravity of his illness, in a rare break with tradition, The Queen personally presented him with the LVO for his work on the Walkway, on the day itself, in the LBC marketing suite.

The following day Robert Shaw was admitted to hospital, and when well enough he continued to administer the affairs of the Trust from his hospital bed, beginning work on the Annual Report. But he did not get better, and on 20 January 1995 he died.

* * * * *

The death of the Chairman was a considerable blow, which left the Trust in a state of flux. Robert Shaw had managed most of the Walkway's business single-handedly. It took some time for his papers to be found and for the Executive to re-form and carry out the Trust's business. One of its first duties was to arrange a memorial service for him. This took place on 4 May at the Queen's Chapel of the Savoy, the chapel of the Royal Victorian Order. The Duke of Gloucester was represented by his Private Secretary, Major Nicholas Barne, the Lord Lieutenant by Illtyd Harrington, and there were addresses by Max Nicholson and Illtyd Harrington. Interestingly, this memorial service appeared to give the Walkway something of a boost.

Meanwhile Neville Labovitch served as acting Chairman and he invited Michael Middleton and William Crossley to join the Executive Committee. At the Annual General Meeting on 27 November Max Nicholson proposed that Neville should become Chairman with Michael Middleton and William Crossley as Vice-Chairmen. Everyone agreed. The Honorary Treasurer, Robert Green, resigned due to ill health (though happily he is still alive at the age of 94 and was recently in touch with the Trust). Geoffrey Price took over his role.

And so began a new era. Neville Labovitch was a businessman and friend of Jeffrey Sterling. He had been involved in the Silver Jubilee when

The Queen at the Opening of The Queen's Walk on 10 November 1994.

he masterminded the Hyde Park Exhibition. He had gone on to help organise the ambitious Great Children's Party in Hyde Park in 1979, when 180,000 children converged on London in celebration of the International Year of the Child. Following the great storm of 1987, The Prince of Wales had asked him to form a committee to raise funds to replant the trees in the Royal Parks. This was successful and the good state of planting in the Royal Parks today owes much to his hard work. Neville was an extraordinary mixture of successful business acumen, imagination and flare, hindered by a certain insecurity. He did not always make friends, though those he befriended were loyal to him to the end. He perceived slights where often there were none. Socially too he was insecure, believing that he did not belong to what he sometimes called 'the magic circle'. This made every event in which he was involved something of a challenge. Yet he had a knack of delivering imaginative events on the day despite all predictions – including his own.

Neville lived in Ennismore Gardens. He was separated from his wife, but devoted to his daughters, both of whom were talented – Carey Labovitch had been voted Young Businesswoman of the Year in 1986 for her creation of *Blitz* magazine. The Walkway entered a new phase.

On 11 October 1995 the Blackfriars underpass (enhanced by a fine slate engraving of a Thames frost) was finally ready and opened by the Lord Mayor of London, Sir Christopher Walford, completing a £1 million project, financed by the two local authorities and nearby businesses. This was the kind of initiative welcomed by the Walkway as it meant that The Queen's Walk became yet more accessible. Pedestrians did not have to climb up and over the bridge, wheelchair users could move easily along it, and it was well lit for additional safety. However, the Trust was disappointed not to be more directly involved or credited with having inspired it.

Towards the end of 1995 news reached Neville Labovitch that President Nelson Mandela was to pay a four-day state visit to London in July 1996. One of Neville's first major coups was to persuade the President to plant a tree in St James's Park early one morning on his State Visit in aid of The Prince of Wales's Royal Parks Tree Appeal and then to unveil a panoramic panel for the Walkway outside South Africa House on 12 July. This event, the finale to the State Visit, attracted the largest ever crowd for a Walkway event, Trafalgar Square literally thronging with people who had come to see the charismatic President in person, where once they stood to protest day after day about his incarceration on Robben Island. The President was accompanied by The Duke of York and Virginia Bottomley, the Duke telling the organisers: 'Don't worry about me – look after him!' This proved an exceptionally high profile event for the Walkway.

But all was not well within the Trust. In February 1997 a Working Party consisting of William Crossley and Michael Middleton produced a document called 'The Way Ahead' to prepare for the 20th anniversary of the Trust. The document came up with various proposals including the need to employ a professional director to deal with maintenance, updating and other new developments. There was £50,000 on deposit. The working group proposed to spend nearly half this on the salary of the director at £15,000 a year for 48 weeks of 25 hours a week. It was proposed that the Honorary Secretary should take on 'a future role in acting as Clerk to the Board of Trustees, including responsibility for all matters concerning the Trust's charitable status.'

The working group seemed sure that if no one would take on the paid role of helping the Chairman and Trustees, the future of the Walkway could not be assured: 'To spend half or more of the Trust's reserves to regain momentum would be a bold step. The alternative, however, is atrophy and the eventual dissolution of the Trust.' On 16 April Neville Labovitch told the Trustees that he was 'in accord with the general tenor of the document' but called an Extraordinary General Meeting at the Mandarin Oriental Hotel, Hyde Park, on 1 May to discuss the various points at issue.

To these proposals Joyce Bellamy registered several objections. On 22 April she told the Chairman and Vice-Chairmen that she did not intend to be at the meeting on 1 May and would step down as Honorary Secretary. She reminded them how she had become involved. The problem had not been the death of Robert Shaw but the loss of the GLC, which had given valuable advice and support, particularly on architectural matters. Even then the London Residuary Body had continued work on The Queen's Walk, and Celia Holmes had arranged much of The Queen's 1994 visit. She did not agree that the Trust had lost momentum when Robert Shaw died. On the contrary, the impact of his memorial service and the Mandela State Visit had showed how resilient the Trust was. As ever she was anxious that the Trust would not get enough technical advice.

There was a lot of to-ing and fro-ing but Joyce was still set to leave on 25 September 1997. But when Diana, Princess of Wales was killed at the end of August, she spotted an early reference to the upcoming Golden Jubilee 'like the proverbial first swallow of summer,' as she put it. This inspired her to launch a new way forward for the Trust, with plans to upgrade the Walkway in time for the Golden Jubilee. She presented a paper on this. Though she was still set to resign as late as 1998, she quietly continued as Honorary Secretary and gradually talk of resignation dissolved under the pressure of work to be done and the characteristic enthusiasm and drive with which she tackled Walkway projects. She also saw and advanced the possibility of the Trust applying for Heritage Lottery funding for its work, a vital help when it materialised.

After considerable discussion and defining of the job description, Chris Patey was appointed as a paid Director reporting to the Executive at six-weekly intervals. In order to do so, he had to step down temporarily as a Trustee.

1997 marked the Golden Wedding of The Queen and The Duke of Edinburgh and the Walkway Trust widened its brief in celebrating Jubilees to include this significant royal milestone. The new panel was placed opposite Buckingham Palace on a new spur of the Walkway, but the unveiling was delayed until the following year, on account of the death of Diana, Princess of Wales.

Another achievement of value was the completion of the Westminster Bridge underpass, considered as important as the Blackfriars Bridge underpass. This was created under the auspices of the London Borough of Lambeth, but again without any recognition for the Walkway, though when Max Nicholson went on Radio 4's *Desert Island Discs* he

Nelson Mandela about to unveil his panel in Trafalgar Square on 12 July 1996.

gave the Walkway good publicity.

In 1998 the Trust changed its name. Having escaped the fate of becoming The London Walkway in 1987, the Trust became the Jubilee Walkway Trust to make it more identifiable with future Jubilees and no longer historically restricted to the Silver Jubilee of 1977. The pavement markers and panoramic panels were examined and the main aim of the Trust was crystallized into having these all restored, repaired and in certain cases renewed in time for The Queen's Golden Jubilee in 2002. Neville Labovitch approached Buckingham Palace and sought The Queen's approval to drop the word 'Silver' from the pavement markers. This was granted.

At this point Jim Walker took note of the Walkway. Jim had been a countryside ranger in Berkshire, an environmental education teacher in the USA and

Jim Walker preparing the Diamond Wedding panel in Parliament Square, 19 November 2007.

a ranger in New Zealand. He had been marketing manager for a company in Australia before returning to Britain, where, between 1992 and 1996, he was Ranger and Nature Conservation Officer in West London, managing forty sites, two environmental education centres, a zoo and a ranger service. For the next two years he was National Trail Manager for the Countryside Agency in Kent and Surrey. He had lately moved from being Manager of the North Downs Way to the London Walking Forum, with an office in the City of London. His mission was to promote walking. His first task was to develop a walking map of London, incorporating the Jubilee Walkway for 26 overseas countries.

Jim contacted Chris Patey who came along for a meeting in his office. Jim told him that he thought he was 'sitting on the best route in London and that more should be done to promote it.' Chris was trying to raise money and contemplating a reprint of the map. Jim offered to put the Walkway into the Mayor's Transport Plan and recognise it as one of six of the most valuable walking routes in the Capital. He was astonished to find that no one at the Trust seemed to have walked the route lately and so he offered to audit it.

Chris put him in touch with Fredi Newton, then running Neville's working life and monitoring matters for him and two weeks later Jim submitted a report on the state of the route. The Walkway was put into the London Tourist Board map and became the key iconic route for walkers in London. Thus began Jim's fruitful involvement with the Trust which continues to this day.

Soon afterwards there was another shake-up within the Trust. Chris Patey had been unwell. He had undergone three operations. On 11 July he had a meeting with Neville Labovitch and Geoff Price (the Honorary Treasurer). In his short phase as Director he had reorganised the Trust's archives, created a database, involved the Marie Curie Cancer Trust in a sponsored walk and made some progress with fundraising for a new map. He was involved with the Millennium Bridge project and plans to extend the Walkway across it, and monitoring developments with the proposed Diana, Princess of Wales Memorial Walk. But he was disturbed by 'a lack of vision and direction' in the Trust. He was aware that it had proved impossible to raise serious funding. As he stepped down, his message was: 'We need some new, younger blood and some succession planning.'

Michael Middleton formally resigned as Vice-Chairman, something he had been trying to do for the previous 18 months. On 3 August he told Neville that he had reached an age 'beyond which I believe people should not remain in this sort of role.' He was convinced that the Chairman needed 'far more active support' than he was able to give. As a result, on 13 August, Neville presented a paper in preparation for a meeting in the House of Commons. By 11 September William Crossley had also stepped down as Vice-Chairman. Chris Patey, Michael Middleton and William Crossley all continued as Trustees and remained supportive to the Walkway. Sir James Swaffield now joined the Executive.

The Buckingham Palace panoramic panel in commemoration of The Queen and The Duke of Edinburgh's Golden Wedding was finally unveiled by The Duke of Gloucester on 28 April 1998.

On 11 June 1999 a meeting was held in the House of Commons to remind the Walkway's many supporters of its existence and to inspire interest in the forthcoming Golden Jubilee. Joyce Bellamy gave a slide presentation to the distinguished representatives present. A further meeting took place at Guildhall in November at which Jim Walker addressed the Trustees and suggested what needed to be done.

These meetings had the effect of injecting new zest into the Trust. Sadly however, Neville Labovitch's chairmanship became less effective because he developed early signs of Pick's Disease, a form of Alzheimer's, which presently made it hard for him to run the Trust as dynamically as he would have wished.

The show was kept on the road thanks to the stalwart work of various figures in the background. Fredi Newton worked with Neville and made sure that the Chairman's business was dealt with, and Joyce Bellamy was, as ever, an energetic Honorary Secretary, attending meetings, forging links, and as she liked to put it, giving people the opportunity to donate their money to Walkway-related enterprises. Being Secretary of the Metropolitan Public Gardens Association provided her with many chances for combined operations.

Fortunately the Trust overcame the difficult circumstances of the Chairman's illness. Though on the outside it appeared that everything was 'full steam ahead', it was not an easy time. It is a great tribute to Fredi and Joyce and to the Trustees that the Trust weathered these grave internal problems.

In 2000 the Walkway was extended by the

A panorama of the Walkway by Rebecca Elliott, 2006.

Tate Modern and Millennium Bridge.

Millennium Spur – running the route along Birdcage Walk in St James's Park to Buckingham Palace and to the panel installed as part of The Queen's Golden Wedding celebrations.

There were a few problems before the Millennium Bridge was able to open to pedestrians. The Walkway crosses it linking Tate Modern and St Paul's Cathedral. The work was greatly helped by grants from the Bridge House Estates Trust. Panoramic panels were added to the bridge in both directions to interpret the views up and down stream.

The Trust ramped up its efforts in 2000. The newly revived Technical Committee reorganised and ratified the actual route taken by the Walkway, improving its route within the City of London, beginning the enlargement of the Bloomsbury spur to link with St Pancras and King's Cross stations, improving road crossing points, particularly in regard to access for the disabled – what is called 'step free'. In St James's Park the route was slightly altered so as not to coincide with the newly introduced Diana, Princess of Wales Memorial route. Panels needed updating. The new goal was the Golden Jubilee of 2002. Everything had to be ready by then.

New panels continued to appear, some with more lasting success than others. The Cheapside panel, paid for by Balls Brothers, was unveiled by Robin Eve, Chief Commoner of the City of London, on 24 May. Originally there had been objection to too much 'clutter' on the pavement there, as since 1996 there had been police control boxes and a 'ring of steel' and it looked as though the panel would have to be placed on the traffic island. Geoffrey Rowley, former Town Clerk and a Trustee, used his city contacts to resolve that problem and four years later it was unveiled. But since then the panel has been destroyed by a truck and not replaced.

Most importantly there was a Congress Luncheon at the House of Commons on 11 September at which Lord Sterling (as Jeffrey Sterling had become) addressed the guests about the origins of the Walkway and reminded the assembled company of the opportunities provided by the fast-approaching Golden Jubilee. Joyce Bellamy again showed slides to explain the development of the Walkway and the environmental audit prepared by the London Walking Forum was also on show. The guests were invited to support the refurbishment of the Walkway and soon afterwards the Brook Trust gave a generous donation and ExxonMobil paid for the updating of their panoramic panel at St Clement Dane's Church.

* * * * *

I was one of two new Trustees confirmed at the meeting of Trustees at Westminster City Hall on 2 November, so I can now give a more personal account of the proceedings. For many years since the Silver Jubilee I had been a close friend of Neville's. He had involved me in the Great Children's Party of 1979, and the event on The Queen's 60th Birthday in April 1986 when children processed en masse up the Mall to present The Queen with daffodils. I had frequently helped Neville with his speeches. It was Fredi's idea to bring me in at this point as it was becoming increasingly difficult for Neville to manage his affairs. The nature of his illness was such that he did not wish to relinquish appointments but Fredi she knew that he would not feel threatened by me. Neville had kept me involved in Walkway events and he had invited me to the Festival Hall when The Queen and The Duke of Edinburgh came in 1988. It was most exciting to be involved with the Walkway again.

The long-term plan (or as it turned out short term) was that I would take over the running of the Trust. Neville would be promoted to President, thus alleviating him of administrative responsibility, Sir James Swaffield, who had been acting as Vice-Chairman for a while, would become Chairman and at the end of the Golden Jubilee year I would succeed him. Neville was happy with his promotion.

In March 2001 Fredi Newton was officially contracted to co-ordinate the work of renovations for the Golden Jubilee, a task she undertook with enthusiasm and effect. She proved a tireless fundraiser and the Walkway's files are packed with copies of the letters she sent out, the generous replies

The panoramic panel at One Poultry.

offering help as well as the negative responses – budgets were tight, no funds were available, they did not assist this kind of project, they were unable to take advantage of this offer, etc. Arup informed the Trust that their contribution would be to ensure that the Millennium Bridge was open between St Paul's Cathedral and Tate Modern.

The Trust was not always in tune with public opinion. For some time it had been monitoring the London Eye, which was opened near Jubilee Gardens by the then Prime Minister, Tony Blair, on 31 December 1999. At one meeting the Trustees were unanimous that its situation near the gardens was wholly unsuitable. Then there was discussion as to whether or not it should be included on panels, since it was clearly only a temporary fixture. As it happens, the Eye is now a well-known London landmark. Like the Eiffel Tower in Paris it is set to stay.

On 8 March 2001 Ken Livingstone, Mayor of London, unveiled a rondel set into the paving of the Walkway near the Eye. This depicted the skyline of London and included natural features for the first time. Shooter's Hill and Hampstead Heath were

The London Eye on The Queen's Walk.

marked since they could be seen from the top of the Eye.

In 2002, the year of The Queen's Golden Jubilee, the Jubilee Walkway was completely refurbished. Missing pavement markers were replaced, panoramic panels were added or updated to reflect changes in London's skyline and dropped pavements were introduced to make the Walkway completely accessible to all who used it, including the disabled.

In the end there was only one place where access proved difficult. A step was removed leading from St Martin's Lane at Goodwin Court and revealed a cavernous cellar, the ownership of which was never established. There was nothing to do but to replace the step. That was literally the only place where a wheelchair could not pass and a slight diversion would be necessary. In the spring the first website was launched.

As so often at moments of rejoicing, there was also sadness. Neville Labovitch died in hospital on 13 April 2002, at the age of 75. His seven-year phase of Chairmanship had been one of great achievement, only marred by his ill health. He had been involved with the Walkway from the start. He all but saw the completion of the refurbishment plan and hopefully he felt that the Trust rested in good hands. Later that year there was a celebration of his life at the Orangery of Kensington Palace at which a message was read out from The Prince of Wales, paying tribute to 'the pleasure that he created for so many people over so many years'.

In August Fredi Newton left her post as co-ordinator and went to live in Crete. She had held matters together when Neville was so ill and done a wonderful job. Thanks to her efforts, funding was in good shape, new sums coming from the Heritage Lottery Fund, which supported a new map and encouraged awareness of the Walkway to be raised in London schools. Jim Walker took over her job and his involvement in the next decade of the Trust's activities was to prove crucial.

During Golden Jubilee year a great number of panoramic panels were unveiled. The Duke of

Gloucester was meant to unveil one at Tower Hill gardens on 9 April, but The Queen Mother died on 30 March, and the ceremony had to be postponed since on that day he was walking in her funeral procession. He came on 30 April instead. It was a little low key – a group of Trustees and a few others lined up and the Duke had had to cross London for this. It occurred to me then that these unveiling ceremonies could be better choreographed. It became a challenge to minimise the time of royal unveilings while insuring that the event was witnessed by as many people as possible and in particular by children. We often tied these in with a reception to make it more fun.

The opportunity arose when The Queen unveiled a panel at One Poultry in the City of London on 24 October. This was the perfect engagement. A huge crowd gathered, the roads were briefly closed, there was a real sense of excitement in the City. The Queen came from an engagement at Guildhall and stepped out of her car to be greeted by a fanfare of trumpets from four Guardsmen. Sir James Swaffield made a short speech and The Queen unveiled the panel and met a few guests. She was given some flowers and

Hugo Vickers, with Arthur Vickers, Lord Sterling, The Queen and Sir James Swaffield after the unveiling at One Poultry on 24 October 2002.

Sir Trevor McDonald at the unveiling on Blackfriars Bridge on 11 June 2002.

a picture and the whole event was accomplished within 15 minutes.

A reception followed in the crypt of St Paul's Cathedral, and after that Jim Swaffield stepped down as Chairman of the Trust. I took over. I was flattered that at the age of nearly 51, the Trustees wanted a 'younger man' to help lead the Trust forward.

Determined to be an active Chairman and conscious that I was reaping the benefits of much already achieved by past Chairmen and Trustees, I tried to be as imaginative and hands on as possible. An early idea was to place gold Walkway discs at various points along the route – two gold discs were placed in the City of London to mark The Queen's visit, one was placed at One Poultry where she unveiled the panel and another near Guildhall where she had lunched after the St Paul's Cathedral Golden Jubilee Service. A further gold disc was placed near London Bridge City to mark The Duke of Gloucester's visit in December. At the One Poultry reception, we gave away miniature versions of these gold discs to our various supporters. These were similar to the miniature silver discs created for earlier events such as the Nelson Mandela unveiling.

As in 1977, I took up my needle and sewed a heavy gold trim onto our unveiling banner to make it more impressive and so that it did not blow away at unveilings – as had nearly happened when Sir Trevor McDonald unveiled a panel on Blackfriars Bridge the previous June. The Queen was the first unveiler to use the newly adorned banner.

I took a keen part in writing the texts for the panels and also much of the Annual Reports. These had improved in look enormously in Neville's time. We now made them more lavish. We also started to commission a special Christmas card each year, some reflecting the activities of the year, at other times reproducing paintings of a scene along the Walkway. We even commissioned a painting of the panel looking down Whitehall from the artist, Arabella Hoare.

Towards the end of 2002, we decided to create the new Golden Jubilee Mall link from Buckingham Palace down the Mall to Horse Guards Approach in commemoration of the Golden Jubilee, when, on 4 June 2002, a crowd of a million people gathered to celebrate The Queen. It was my wife Elizabeth (Mouse) who noticed that this significant route (where the key celebrations had taken place) was mysteriously not part of our route. Uniquely this part of the Walkway was marked by a series of gold discs in the ground the length of the Mall.

There came an opportunity for the unveiling of a double panel when The Queen was returning from the Coronation anniversary service at Westminster Abbey on 2 June 2003. At the reconnoitre I asked the Assistant Private Secretary what time The Queen would be with us. He said about 12.35 and I smiled because I knew that that was exactly the moment The Queen was crowned fifty years before. I was able to say this in my short speech. I remember that President de Gaulle had stood up to salute his wartime office, 4 Carlton Gardens, on the state drive to Buckingham Palace in May 1960. I had seen this as a child. The Queen confirmed that she remembered this no doubt worrying act of the General's.

We were joined by Louisa Harrington, a nine-year old girl with a life-threatening illness whose parents had contacted the Make-A-Wish Foundation and told them it was her wish to be a princess for a day and to meet The Queen. We were delighted to have her and ordered a magnificent floral representation of the Crown to be made for her to present. It was so big that Louisa needed to be assisted by her sister. Watched by her parents, she presented this floral crown to The Queen. After The Queen left by car, Louisa left in a special carriage. Towards the end of July, sadly, Louisa died.

Lady Soames, Sir Winston Churchill's daughter, came to the Royal Exchange to unveil a triangular panel. When it was being put in a hole was dug which exposed the tube trains running underneath. This was speedily filled.

Thanks to Jim Walker, the Jubilee Walkway was recognised as one of six Strategic Walks in the Mayor's first Transport Plan. The strategic borough partnership 'Walk London,' led by the City of London, then coordinated a significant investment programme in the Walkway in order to meet the Mayor's commitment to 'complete' the Walkway by 2012.

2003 was also the year that the Trust lost Max Nicholson, creator of the Walkway and its honorary Adviser. He died aged 98 on 26 April. He had attended meetings of the Trust well into his nineties, and fortunately I was able to send a message to him informing him of the Mall extension shortly before he died. He greeted the news with a smile. Our handsome unveiling banner was placed over Max's coffin at his funeral.

Just over a year later, on 12 July 2004, on what would have been Max Nicholson's 100th birthday, a panel outside the National Gallery was unveiled in his memory by The Duke of Gloucester. This was a rather different panel to the normal ones, having been specially designed by Lord Foster of Thames Bank, OM. There was then a reception in the rooftop restaurant of the National Portrait Gallery. The Duke of Gloucester had the chance for a quick tour of some of the exhibitions before he left. Since then, each year on the anniversary of Max's birthday, his son Piers has arranged a memorial walk around part of the Walkway. When possible Trustees have joined this walk, a chance to meet, walk and chat informally, rounding off the excursion in a London pub.

The Queen about to receive a floral crown from Louisa Harrington and her sister, after the Mall unveiling, 2 June 2003.

In 2005 the Trust was commended for Best Community or Partnership Initiative, as part of the London Planning Awards. This recognised achievement in planning across the Capital. The Mayor of London, Ken Livingstone, presented the certificate to me as Chairman at a ceremony at City Hall on 6 December and at the reception afterwards we engaged him in a spirited discussion of many issues involving London and the Walkway, finding him extraordinarily well informed.

In July 2005 it was announced that the 2012 Olympic Games would be held in London. The Trust was already considering how to celebrate the Diamond Jubilee of The Queen in the same year.

It is impossible to pinpoint exactly how an idea forms, especially if it is successful as then numerous people claim it as their own – 'Success has many fathers, Failure has none', as the cliché has it. What is certain is that the idea to create a new route developed in a conversation between Jim

The Countess of Wessex with Hugo Vickers after she unveiled the Queen's 80th birthday panel at Horse Guards on 17 January 2007.

Walker and myself. The moment the Games were won for London, Jim was involved in advising how the Olympic sites could be reached on foot or on bicycles. So we conceived the idea of a Diamond Jubilee Olympic Trail. With a little thought and moulding, this developed into the Jubilee Greenway and work was soon progressing towards its mapping and creation. By 2006 the plans were well advanced.

The idea was to develop and promote this route separately from the original Walkway, though happily, the route coincides with the Walkway along The Queen's Walk.

2007 proved to be an unexpectedly exciting year. We had two exceptional royal visits, first on 17 January when The Countess of Wessex unveiled a panoramic panel to commemorate The Queen's 80th birthday (on 21 April 2006). The panel was placed at Horse Guards. This panel was important as it showed the scene of Trooping the Colour – the first time an actual scene had been recreated on a panel,

rather than architectural features. We arranged Guards to sound a fanfare when The Countess of Wessex arrived. Jim Walker was surprised to see them relaxing beforehand with sandwiches in their bearskins. Major-General Sebastian Roberts, Major-General Commanding the Household Division, entertained us in his office, formerly used by the great Duke of Wellington and still containing his desk.

Later in the year The Queen and The Duke of Edinburgh jointly unveiled a panel in Parliament Square to commemorate their Diamond Wedding. This engagement fitted the established criterion – minimum time expended by The Queen, maximum exposure. I wrote to the Private Secretary inviting Her Majesty after the Diamond Wedding Thanksgiving Service in Westminster Abbey. Though the actual anniversary was on 20 November, the service was held on 19 November because The Queen and Prince Philip were leaving for Malta and a Commonwealth meeting in Uganda. The Private Secretaries were thinking of something else that could be done that day and, fortunately for us, they chose our unveiling.

It was a wet morning, a council truck passing backwards and forwards sucking up the water from

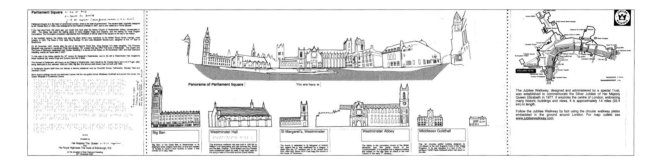

The design for the Parliament Square panel, with Braille features.

the puddles. We all got roundly soaked in at least one downpour. The question arose – overcoats or no overcoats. At the last moment we heard that the Royal Family were not wearing them while ours were looking bedraggled. Within our pen there was a telephone box and this swiftly became the depository for a number of soggy coats. Luckily the sun came out just in time for the actual ceremony.

The Duke of Gloucester came over from the Abbey after the service and The Queen and The Duke of Edinburgh arrived in the royal Bentley. The panoramic panel marked a significant development in the type of panels we would produce in the future. It contained a considerable Braille element to make it more accessible to the partially sighted. One feature was a telephone number that could be rung. Then a message described the view that could be seen with historical information. On the panel itself the significant landmarks were done in Braille, so that, for example, a partially sighted person could 'see' Big Ben for the first time. Isobella Murdoch, partially sighted, explained this feature to The Queen and Duke. Prince Philip was exercised by the panel wanting to know why the ground was curved. He was finally satisfied when Jim Walker explained that by this method it was possible to include a wider vista.

To this ceremony I invited Michael Middleton, by then in a nursing home following a serious stroke. I presented him to The Queen, hoping that this would make him something of a star back in the home and also to show loyalty to those who had helped us in the past. Having a young family, it was nice that my daughter Alice presented flowers to The Queen and her twin brother, George, gave a framed photograph to the Duke. Their elder brother, Arthur, had given

The Queen flowers at One Poultry in 2002, and he too was there that day.

The unveiling was filmed live on BBC 24, and attracted considerable coverage in the national press. After The Queen left, The Duke of Gloucester joined our guests at a reception in the crypt of Westminster Abbey, by kind permission of the Dean of Westminster, and introduced the Trust's ideas for the Jubilee Greenway. We loved this day, which combined the formality of the morning with the more relaxed reception, guests drinking and children scampering around.

Most of the Jubilee Greenway already existed, but the plan was to make it safer and pleasanter and one which would help people get to the Olympic venues, whether on foot, on bicycles, or in some cases even on horseback. Jim Walker selected and mapped out the way it would go (some 60 kilometres round London) and mustered enthusiastic support from the London boroughs through which the Greenway passed. Work began in earnest. In 2008 the Jubilee Greenway was officially adopted by the new Mayor of London as a 7th Strategic Route, which allowed further support for the completion and promotion of the new route via the Walk London strategic partnership.

The Jubilee Walkway itself remained in good condition and we improved it quietly in a variety of ways, not least in donating benches, planting trees, and where appropriate placing new panoramic panels and updating existing ones.

* * * * *

The Mile End loop of the Jubilee Greenway.

There was a memorable day in May 2008 when Jim Walker and I took to bicycles and he showed me the proposed route so that I could write about it for the new website to be devoted to the Greenway. Information was needed in respect of the way it went and the historical and interesting sites encountered along the way. To begin with, we noted directions: 'Turn right . . . turn left', but I soon realised that that would take for ever. So I asked Jim to show me the way, promising to return on my own and take notes later.

We set off from Queensway and pressed on to Paddington, Little Venice, along the Regent's Canal, to Camden Market and on to Victoria Park in the East End. This led on to the actual Greenway and my first glimpse of the Olympic site at Stratford. On we went through Beckton District Park, past the old docks and City Airport, and over the ferry to Woolwich. At this point there was no alternative but to cycle home along the south bank of the Thames, some 60 kilometres achieved in a day. Having

resisted bicycling since I was in my twenties, it was something of a shock to the system, but had proved immensely interesting.

Later in the year I returned to different sections on foot, one day walking from Kensington to Little Venice, taking a narrow boat to Camden Market and then following the route to Victoria Park and down to Limehouse. Thus I got to know the Jubilee Greenway, learning much about the history of London as I walked. Some of these walks were amongst my happiest days in 2008.

On 8 September The Duke of Gloucester hosted a meeting in the Chinese Dining Room at Buckingham Palace, the room which Queen Victoria decorated with details from George IV's Brighton Pavilion. It was in this room that The Queen had made her famous broadcast the night before the funeral of Diana, Princess of Wales. Here we formally laid out our plans to a committee of distinguished representatives from organisations with an interest in the Olympics and the route itself. They were selected just as Jeffrey Sterling had selected his Committee at the time of the 1977 Jubilee and several times we called on them for help in the next few years.

It was a good time to encourage walking. The Government had lately recognised that every £1 given to walking saved the National Health Service some £7, thus funding was more readily available for walking projects than for some other organisations.

It could be argued that the Jubilee Greenway had been launched on several occasions. I spoke of it when The Countess of Wessex unveiled the Horse Guards panel, it was launched again in the crypt of Westminster Abbey and there was the meeting at the Palace. It was then officially launched in public by The Duke of Gloucester when he spent a day in the East End on 30 April 2009. He began by visiting the Abbey Mills Pumping Station, then cycled along the Greenway to the Olympic site where members of the press were gathered.

There was an entertaining moment when our Treasurer, John Polk, was presented with a particular bicycle. He had been misidentified as the Duke. Opposite the great Olympic stadium, speeches were made, some of which appeared on the local London television news that evening. The Duke then toured the Olympic site, still very much in embryo form, but advancing steadily. There was so much activity that it was reminiscent of the last scene in a James Bond movie, little trucks moving about purposefully. The Duke was taken to Victoria Park where lunch was served and many Trustees gathered. After that the party moved onto a long boat and travelled up the Regent's Canal to Islington. Here too there was some drama. Several Trustees and the Duke had to move inside swiftly as the boat approached a lock and it was clear that at any moment water would gush into the boat as presently it did. This was a full and most enjoyable day.

The Greenway developed rapidly. Jim Walker brought Jenny Humphreys in to work with the Trust. She had spent nine years working in Corporate Communications in London, walked the Inca Trail in Peru and the Cornish coastal path, rowed at Henley and sang as a soprano with the City of London Choir and Quorum Choir. She joined Jim's team at Walk England and to her fell the onerous task of dealing with the local authorities over planning issues, including the placing of each

ABOVE The Duke of Gloucester on the bicycle ride in April 2009.

BELOW Jenny Humphreys with the first Greenway disc on the Broad Walk in Kensington Gardens.

of the 500 or so marker discs, every one requiring discussion, some more so than others. This kept her busy for the next three years. One borough proved especially difficult when it seemed we might have to apply for individual planning permission for each of 70 markers. Fortunately we were rescued by one of our Committee members.

During these years the bulk of the work of the Trust was done differently than it had been years before. We still had executive meetings and meetings of Trustees, but the day-to-day administration was conducted by email, quick phone calls and occasional meetings over coffee and sometimes wine. Jim Walker was the perfect director/coordinator. He would present me with a long list of things that needed to be done and then highlight the absolute essentials. Likewise he proved adept at turning dreams and seemingly impossible plans into reality.

Not everything went well. There was a worrying period when the Trust was involved in a serious misunderstanding relating to VAT. This was resolved by the immediate admission of the mistake and its resolution (but not without inevitable administrative costs). By and large though, the atmosphere was totally positive and a lot of our conversations were conducted amidst laughter, and no meeting of the Trustees passed by without a share of good-hearted repartee. I suppose that this was because we were all moving forward and by chance the team worked well together, surely the essential for an endeavour of this kind.

When the final event of the Trust was being arranged, the emails went to and fro with terrifying rapidity. Jenny Humphreys pointed out that she, Jim and I were all 'control freaks'. I replied that this may well be true but equally we were 'deferential control freaks' since we seemed always willing to accept a better plan when it was suggested.

In 2009 the Environmental or Greening Committee was created in order to further promote and direct the work that Joyce Bellamy had been undertaking with such determination and for so many years. Their important achievements are listed in Appendix 1.

On 27 April 2010 the Annual General Meeting of the Trust was held at the Guoman Tower Hotel at St Katharine Docks, after which a bench was unveiled in memory of Peter Drew, a founder Trustee who had done so much for St Katharine Docks and who had died in 2007. Sir James Swaffield recalled that when The Queen visited the dock in 1977 it was Peter who persuaded the local schools to fill the scene with children. Peter's widow, Wendy, gave a reception at an Italian restaurant and from that vantage point people could be seen seated on Peter's bench as if it had been there for ever.

Geoffrey Rowley attended this occasion. To the shock of his fellow Trustees, the following night he was killed crossing the road when returning to his home in Woodford Green from an evening function in the City. It was some consolation that he had clearly been very happy on the last full day of his life.

* * * * *

Mindful of the considerable role that Charles Wintour and the *Evening Standard* had played in promoting the 1977 Silver Jubilee, I pressed the Editor, Geordie Greig, to let me write a piece in the *Standard* urging Londoners to support the Diamond Jubilee and giving news of the developing Greenway. This was published on 7 April 2010 as a result of which Transport for London renewed their interest in the Greenway and volunteered considerable funding so that we could complete the route. Under the circumstances I was quite happy not to have received a fee for writing this article.

A new panel was placed in Trafalgar Square looking down Whitehall. We invited Robert Davis, Leader of Westminster City Council and a former Lord Mayor of Westminster, to unveil it. Unfortunately the day chosen, 30 November, coincided with early snow and a gathering of unruly students intent on marching to Westminster. Luckily just before the appointed hour, the police closed Whitehall and a Pied Piper worked out that the students could reach Westminster via Admiralty Arch. They all followed him like sheep and the moment the coast was clear, we quickly covered the panel with our banner, Robert performed the ceremony, we shook hands for a photograph and we sped off to the sanctity of the National Portrait Gallery.

By 2011 the Walkway was well maintained and in good condition. The Greenway was nearly finished. As ever there were last minute hitches. In the late summer Jenny Humphreys heard that the makers of the Greenway glass markers had gone into liquidation. With great presence of mind, she rescued the stock just before the receivers closed in.

* * * * *

After the royal unveiling of 2007 I had promised Sir Christopher Geidt, The Queen's Private Secretary, that I would go quiet but I warned him that I would pop up again when the Diamond Jubilee loomed. He was not entirely surprised to hear this. In the summer of 2011 negotiations opened with Buckingham Palace when I invited The Queen to open the completed Jubilee Greenway. Presently news came that she had agreed to unveil a special Greenway marker outside Buckingham Palace. At once we commissioned a gold collar to surround this disc, reminding passers-by that this celebrated the Diamond Jubilee of The Queen, was part of a 60-kilometre route and an initiative of the Trust.

For some time it had become apparent that the work of the Trust was all but done. There was good funding for the two routes which would carry us into 2012, but after that, with no obvious opportunities for expanding our existing routes and the opportunities for the kind of funding we had enjoyed being now greatly limited, there would be less to do. I wondered what a new Chairman could hope to achieve if he took over my job.

I consulted Jim Swaffield and after securing his blessing, it was put to the Trustees that we should wind up the Trust and hand the two routes over to Jim's social enterprise, Walk England, so that he could maintain and promote them. The Trustees agreed unanimously. This decision in no way diminished the original aims of the Trust. It was just a better way forward. Having worked with Jim with nothing but enjoyment for ten years, I was delighted when he invited me to take the Chair of Walk England. Part of my remit was to keep an eye on our two routes.

Even as the Trust wound down, there were more panels in the offing, in particular two in Parliament Square, funded by the Supreme Court. One celebrates the Royal Wedding of 29 April 2011, when Prince William married Catherine Middleton, replacing the panel opposite the Queen Elizabeth II Conference Centre. The other panel, this time with a political theme, replaces the one outside St Margaret's, Westminster.

The Walkway had come a long way since its inception in 1977. The Trust had enjoyed moments of prosperity and lurched through its lean times too. Throughout those years the determination of key Trustees had kept it going. The Jubilee Walkway has given a lot of pleasure to Londoners and to overseas visitors and as the anniversary of the Diamond Jubilee arrived, the Jubilee Greenway was ready to join it. The Trustees met formally for the last time on 2 February 2012.

* * * * *

2012 was a Leap Year. All through the month of February BBC Radio 4's PM programme had a campaign urging its listeners to find something unusual and really special to do on 29 February. It would have been hard to beat the day enjoyed by the Trust. In advance of it every aspect of the ceremony at the Palace was tried and tested. The Queen was to unveil the first and last disc right in the middle of the central gates of Buckingham Palace. The challenge was to make it easier for her to do so. Year after year the Queen Mother laid a cross at the Festival of Remembrance outside Westminster Abbey, stooping down with increasing difficulty to place her cross on the ground. Only when she was 100 did someone have the bright idea of putting a rostrum in front of her, so that she could place it on that.

Jim Walker and his 16-year-old son, Ben, designed a splendid frame to go over the disc. This had four fleurs-de-lis at each corner, and a representation of the Jubilee Walkway crown on top. It was made at a local forge. It proved handsome and eye-catching and hopefully set a worrying precedent for future royal unveilings by other organisations.

The next problem was the banner. Jim and I spent

an hour or so trying out every possible combination of flag and banner since I still had ten or so from 1977. Our large one got stuck on the spikes of the crown. Others fell to the ground in a slightly undignified way. In the end we settled on a small banner on the ground with a large red trim and a long cord. I bought the trim and cord and spent a weekend, as thirty-five years earlier, lining the banner and stitching on the trim and cord.

The day dawned. Crowds gathered expecting to see the Changing of the Guard though uniquely this was delayed by 12 minutes or so. The disc was already set in the ground. The crowds were amazed to realise that besides the Guards and the bands they were to be rewarded by the rare sight of The Queen outside her Palace. Our Trustees and guests gathered and presently I went in to the Palace to find The Duke of Gloucester who had arrived by

LEFT The specially created banner and frame for the Opening of the Jubilee Greenway, Buckingham Palace on 29 February 2012.

BELOW Crowds waiting for the Changing of the Guard, excited to see The Queen.

56

The Queen unveiling the Buckingham Palace Greenway disc. Left to Right: Jim Walker, Jenny Humphreys, The Duke of Edinburgh, The Duke of Gloucester, The Queen and Hugo Vickers.

car. There was a royal salute in the form of half the National Anthem as he crossed the forecourt.

Presently the royal Bentley arrived and The Queen and Prince Philip stepped out. I presented Jim Walker and Jenny Humphreys first as they had done all the work between them. Then the Trustees were presented in order of appointment. I made a short speech and then invited The Queen to unveil the disc. All the preparation, practising and rehearsals paid off. The unveiling was achieved smoothly and with poise. Jim and Jenny then told the Royal Family how the discs had been made, Jim's six-year-old son Noah presented The Queen with flowers and The Queen and The Duke of Edinburgh left. 'Are you going to walk it then?' was Prince Philip's parting shot. I assured him I had walked every inch of it which seemed to please him.

The formal part of the day over, the invited guests were taken by bus to Westminster Pier where they embarked in *Golden Jubilee*. The Duke of Gloucester had already arrived on board and Commander John

Ludgate, one of London's Deputy Lieutenants, was looking after him. Champagne was served as *Golden Jubilee* set off downstream. Everyone then had lunch at tables of six as we passed through the changing riverscape of London.

We disembarked at Limehouse and set off in two LOCOG buses to the Olympic Park where we were given a tour of the fantastic site ready and waiting for the great games in the summer. We then proceeded to the corner nearest Stratford High Street and the Bazalgette Greenway, along which our route passes.

Here, at what will become the gateway to Queen Elizabeth Olympic Park after the 2012 London Olympic Games was the lit feature – sixty lit discs designed as 'E II R' surmounted by a crown, set into the ground. Over this thousands of visitors will in

The Duke of Gloucester hoisting a Silver Jubilee flag in the Olympic Park at the site of the E II R lit feature on 29 February 2012.

due course enter the park and at twilight they willl light up as people pass over them. This feature, like the Greenway disc symbol, was impressively designed by Jim Walker.

The Duke of Gloucester raised one of the Jubilee flags next to it and made a short valedictory speech. The Jubilee Greenway had been given the most magnificent opening. The route was complete; our task was done. In the group of sixty or so guests were many who had helped create it at a variety of different levels over the past six years. Amongst them seven or eight had been involved in the London Celebrations Committee as long ago as 1977.

In the distance the skyline of new London bore features such as the Shard and the Gherkin representing a world sometimes hard to understand, a world far in time and space from the London of 1977. Symbolically, the Jubilee Walkway and the Jubilee Greenway had crossed many miles. So too had they and we travelled through 35 years in time. It was the end of a long journey.

As he left, The Duke of Gloucester mused: 'I suppose you are now going to burst into tears?' I replied: 'I might.'

Route of the Jubilee Walkway

INTRODUCTION

The original Silver Jubilee Walkway began in Leicester Square, marked in 1977 by a column surmounted by a Jubilee crown. From there it made its way through Trafalgar Square and St James's Park to the Houses of Parliament. It crossed Lambeth Bridge and continued along the South Bank of the Thames past County Hall, the new Jubilee Gardens (on the former Festival of Britain site, lately a car park), all the way to Tower Bridge. It crossed Tower Bridge and ended at All Hallows-by-the-Tower.

In those early days the Walkway was still somewhat unsatisfactory since there were numerous detours from the side of the river. To enjoy river views at all points was an ambitious aim, tempered with the delicate balance between such a route and the need not to upset the natural wildlife by the river. A great many riparian stretches were opened as redevelopment occurred, this being a firm condition in planning permissions granted by County Hall, each case considered individually – sometimes a long and complicated process.

Originally the route was marked with markers in metal frames, with the logo of the London Celebrations Committee – St Paul's Cathedral within a Gothic crown, made of coloured epoxy resin, as inserts. These proved to be adversely affected by sunlight, and disintegrated. Sometimes they were vandalised. So they were replaced with 300 aluminium plaques.

The nature of the walk is such that the walker can start and finish wherever he likes. These days the walker can download maps for different routes. It offers fabulous views and aspects both architectural and horticultural. By walking it, London can be discovered and in so doing the walker can gently maintain and improve his or her health.

Over the years the Walkway has been extended from the Tower of London through the City and back to Leicester Square. A loop was created at St Katharine Docks, two additional loops were added encompassing Bloomsbury and the City, after the Golden Jubilee in 2002 the Walkway was extended up the Mall.

ABOVE AND BELOW Leicester Square. The statue of Charlie Chaplin was unveiled by Sir Ralph Richardson in 1981.

LEFT Nelson's Column dominates Trafalgar Square.

Section 1 – The Western Loop

Leicester Square is now wholly pedestrianised and until recently contained markers set in the ground indicating the various countries of the Commonwealth and their distance from this point in London. The route leads out via the southwest corner next to the Odeon West End Cinema and heads south down St Martin's Street passing Westminster Library on the left and the between two parts of the National Gallery into Trafalgar Square.

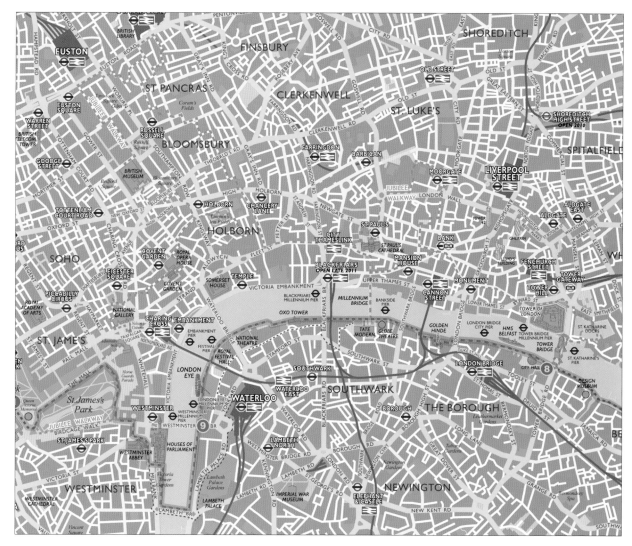

Trafalgar Square was laid out in 1840 by Sir Charles Barry, the architect of the new Houses of Parliament. It is now a 'World Square' and well known as a place of national rejoicing, the celebration of New Year's Eve as well as political demonstrations. Until recently it was the home of thousands of pigeons. It is dominated by Nelson's Column with its 18 metre statue of Admiral Lord Nelson on top of the 171 metre column, put there to mark his victory at Trafalgar.

Next to the National Gallery is the National Portrait Gallery, opened in 1856. For a long time it was a slightly moribund repository of old portraits of historically famous people in Britain (some of which were undeniably splendid), but in the 1960s, under

the directorship of Sir Roy Strong, it was revitalised and now stages exhibitions of photography and is to the forefront of national artistic life.

The Walkway passes under Admiralty Arch, the next landmark, now an office but formerly the old Admiralty building. It was designed by Sir Aston Webb in 1912 and is one of the great ceremonial arches of London. It leads into the Mall which was laid out as an avenue in 1660-62 when Charles II redesigned St James's Park. The Mall is the ceremonial route of London, leading to Buckingham Palace. The Queen and The Duke of Edinburgh travelled along it from the Palace in the Gold State Coach to the Coronation at Westminster Abbey in 1953 and to St Paul's Cathedral for the

Thanksgiving Services for the Silver Jubilee in 1977 and the Golden Jubilee in 2002.

The Walkway begins on the right hand side of the Mall passing the Royal Marines Memorial and passes in front of Carlton House Terrace. It crosses the road opposite the Duke of York steps, with its large granite column and bronze statue of the Duke and enters St. James's Park.

This route leads down Horse Guards Approach, passing the Cavalry War Memorial and Horse Guards Parade. By the road there is a panel showing the scene for Trooping the Colour, held every June to mark The Queen's official birthday. The route continues past 10 Downing Street (official residence of the Prime Minister) on the left and reaches Birdcage Walk.

Section 5 heads to the right to Buckingham Palace.

The route leads into Great George Street and Parliament Square. Here are Big Ben and the Palace of Westminster, Westminster Abbey and the Supreme Court. The square contains statues of many famous statesmen, including Sir Winston Churchill and Nelson Mandela. Bombs blew out the windows of Westminster Hall during World War II and twisted the sword held by the statue of Richard Coeur de Lion.

The Walkway passes between St Margaret's, Westminster, and the Palace of Westminster, formerly the residence of Kings. The clock tower contains the famous Big Ben bell, cast in 1858 and named after Benjamin Hall, Commissioner of Works at that time. The Walkway leads past Victoria Tower and then turns into Victoria Tower Gardens, where The Queen planted an oak tree in February 1977 to mark her Silver Jubilee.

Lambeth Bridge takes the Walkway over to the South Bank which it follows all the way to Tower Bridge. All the way along this part it stays as close to the Thames as possible, only veering away at one point at Southwark. At Westminster the route becomes The Queen's Walk, extending along the South Bank from Westminster Bridge to Tower Bridge.

There is no doubt that The Queen's Walk was the greatest achievement of the Jubilee Walkway Trust. It took until 1994 to open up the many riparian sections. This is now a vibrant part of London, greatly enjoyed by Londoners and tourists alike. Even on a cold Sunday evening, where as late as the 1960s it would be a mass of forbidding warehouses, it hums with people enjoying life in wine bars and

ABOVE The Jubilee Gardens, London Eye, the Shell Building and County Hall.

RIGHT Lambeth Palace, home of the Archbishop of Canterbury.

restaurants or just walking along it.

The skyline of London has changed dramatically in the last half century, and continues to change from year to year, particularly along this section of the Thames. It has changed less at Lambeth than further down the river, the Houses of Parliament occupying much of the view across the river between Lambeth Bridge and Westminster Bridge.

Before 1750 the Thames only had one bridge, the famous London Bridge which had indeed fallen down on a number of occasions. Bridges were then built in relatively quick succession – the original Westminster Bridge in 1750, Lambeth Bridge in 1862, Tower Bridge in 1886 and Chelsea Bridge in 1888. The first Waterloo Bridge (1811-17) was designed by John Rennie (1794-1874), but destroyed in 1934. The latest London Bridge was built as recently as 1972.

In the olden days there used to be penny steamers that plied their way between Chelsea and Woolwich, departing every 15 minutes, and stopping at some 27 piers. These were withdrawn in 1908. Road travel became safer and more popular, road surfaces being improved by the Metropolitan Board of Works in 1856 and the LCC in 1889.

The first landmark is the Museum of Garden History, based in a disused church. This Museum was helped into creation with a grant at the time of The Queen's Silver Jubilee. It stands next to Lambeth Palace, the official London residence of the

Archbishop of Canterbury.

On the South Bank stands St Thomas' Hospital, originally founded early in the 12th century as part of the Priory of St Mary Overie (rededicated to St Thomas the Martyr and then to St Thomas the Apostle). The Florence Nightingale Museum is tucked behind the hospital, to the southwest of Westminster Bridge. This museum is particularly popular with primary schools as the career of the nursing pioneer Florence Nightingale (1820-1910) is part of the national syllabus. Almost in view is Waterloo Station in Lambeth, which serves the South West and West Country. Until 2007 the Eurostar left from here.

Westminster Bridge links Lambeth and Westminster. The first bridge was built in 1750 and replaced in 1862. It bears an heraldic plaque commemorating Queen Victoria and Prince Albert. From the earlier stone Westminster Bridge, William Wordsworth was inspired to write his 1802 sonnet: 'Earth has not anything to show more fair'.

The route continues along the South Bank past County Hall, the former home of the Greater London Council and London County Council until 1986. Designed by Ralph Knott, it has since been converted into a number of different enterprises. Part of it is a Marriott Hotel. The London Aquarium, Dalí Universe, the Moiveum of London and other outlets are also contained in that great building.

Next comes the now famous London Eye. It is the world's highest observation wheel and offers passengers amazing views of London. The Eye takes guests on a 30-minute flight, rising to 135m above the Thames. It has 32 high-tech fully enclosed capsules in which the passengers travel. The Eye is now so symbolic of London that it was the site of the fabulous firework display to herald the New Year 2011/2012. Near it is a Jubilee Walkway rondel showing the distant views that might be observed from the Eye on a clear day.

Jubilee Gardens, next to the Eye, were landscaped on the site of the Festival of Britain between County Hall and Royal Festival Hall, as the major environmental initiative of the London Celebrations Committee for The Queen's Silver Jubilee in 1977. The site had previously been a stone manufactory,

The National Theatre on the South Bank.

a brewery, a glassworks, a warehouse, a helicopter pad, and a car park. (A famous photograph of this was taken from the top of the Shell Centre in the exceptionally cold winter of 1963, showing the tracks made by the cars in the snow).

The gardens cost £300,000 to restore and were officially opened by The Queen on the night of 9 June 1977 just after she opened the Walkway. The gardens suffered when the Jubilee Line was excavated beneath them, but in time for the Diamond Jubilee in 2012 they have again been imaginatively restored. Behind the gardens is the Shell Centre with its 24 floors. Between Jubilee Gardens and the river stands the huge Silver Jubilee flagpole, raised there early one morning in the year of The Queen's Silver Jubilee in 1977.

Crossing the Thames is Jubilee Bridge, a railway bridge with pedestrian bridges either side built to celebrate The Golden Jubilee in 2002, and opened by HRH Princess Alexandra. There are four Jubilee Walkway panels on these bridges, interpreting the view in both directions on the Thames.

After the war the Royal Festival Hall was built on the site of the Lion (or Red Lion) Brewery at Lambeth, which was demolished in 1949. It stands at the heart of Southbank Centre complex and was opened in 1951 as part of the Festival of Britain. The hall is one of the world's leading concert venues. Next to it is Queen Elizabeth Hall, the second largest concert hall on site, for chamber orchestras, quartets, choirs, dance performances and opera.

The Millennium Bridge with St Paul's Cathedral in the background.

There are also the Purcell Room (the most intimate concert hall, suitable for chamber music, literary and spoken word events, mime and solo recitals) and the Front Room. The Hayward Gallery is a gallery for the visual arts.

The National Film Theatre has three screens and offers a programme of films from the British Film Institute archive as well as screening new releases not being shown elsewhere. Next to all these is the South Bank book market, selling a wide range of books at competitive prices.

The National Theatre was designed by Sir Denys Lasdun and opened by The Queen in 1976. In 2007 a statue was unveiled to the actor, Laurence Olivier. It looks towards Waterloo Bridge, the title of a much-admired 1940 film starring his second wife (and the love of his life) – Vivien Leigh.

Moving along, there is the London TV Centre (the South Bank studio from where the *Daybreak* morning breakfast programme and many other such programmes are broadcast).

The Walkway passes Gabriel's Wharf, the OXO Tower and under Blackfriars Bridge, passing Bankside Gallery, before reaching Tate Modern, in the former Bankside Power Station, which houses Britain's collection of international modern and contemporary art. The gallery was converted to contain four wings featuring Surrealism, Minimalism, post-war abstraction in Europe and the United States, and the three linked movements of Cubism, Futurism and Vorticism.

Outside it is Millennium Bridge, the latest bridge to cross the Thames. It was designed by Foster & Partners and developed in close collaboration with the sculptor Sir Anthony Caro. The bridge appears as a thin ribbon of steel by day. At night it is illuminated and gives the impression of a shining blade of light across the river. The opening of the bridge was not without controversy since it was deemed unsafe and there were delays while this was sorted out. The Millennium Bridge crosses the Thames, linking Tate Modern to St Paul's Cathedral. Cross the Thames on the Millennium Bridge.

Section 2 of the Walkway continues along the South Bank, the original route of the Walkway.

From outside Tate Modern there is a fine view of St Paul's Cathedral. The Cathedral stands on the

ABOVE The house Sir Christopher Wren lived in on the South Bank when St Paul's Cathedral was being built.

RIGHT St Paul's Cathedral.

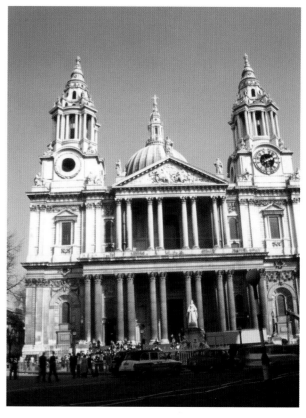

summit of Ludgate Hill, and though now dwarfed by recent building work, can still be seen clearly from The Queen's Walk. The original St Paul's was dedicated in 604 and a larger edifice built by William the Conqueror in 1087. By the 17th century it had become somewhat dilapidated. It was completely destroyed in the Great Fire of London in 1666.

Sir Christopher Wren built the present Cathedral when living opposite on the South Bank, affording him the chance to supervise his work. The dome, when built, was the world's second largest, after St Peter's in Rome.

In the crypt are buried many famous people including Wren himself, Admiral Lord Nelson, the 1st Duke of Wellington and the artist, JMW Turner. The state funeral of Sir Winston Churchill took place here on 30 January 1965, and in July 1981, The Prince of Wales married Lady Diana Spencer, an event which was televised and seen by 750 million people across the globe. The Queen Mother celebrated her 80th and 100th birthdays here in 1980 and 2000 respectively, and Jubilees have been celebrated in the Cathedral – Queen Victoria riding here in a carriage in 1897 for her Diamond Jubilee (the service held on the steps as she was too lame to descend from the carriage in public). King George V celebrated his Silver Jubilee with a service here in 1935, and the present Queen celebrated her Silver Jubilee here in 1977, her Golden Jubilee in 2002 and

Diamond Jubilee in 2012.

Until 1939 the northern shore of the Thames between Blackfriars and Tower Bridge was filled with working warehouses of some antiquity. All along the South Bank were wharves and warehouses with great cranes (that dipped in salute to the coffin of Sir Winston Churchill as it was conveyed up the Thames from Tower Pier after the State Funeral in January 1965).

St Paul's Wharf was demolished in 1898 and Queenhithe Dock, the oldest dock in the city, which dated to Saxon times, was likewise demolished in 1971 and a tourist hotel built on the site. At St Katharine Docks (the dock that was saved), one of Philip Hardwick's warehouses was rescued. Now St Katharine's Wharf sports a marina for smart yachts.

In 1710 St Paul's Cathedral stood high above every building in its vicinity. Today, like the Tower of London, it is all but swamped by glass buildings and skyscrapers. In 1883 the architect A.H. Mackmurdo praised the Cathedral: 'I know of no more magnificent sight . . . this view of London wrapt in the dark-halo of each cloud . . . the pale cathedral lifting itself aloft – a miracle of unmoved dignity, boldly central among her square massive mansions, and huge blocks of seven-storied offices.'

After the Great Fire of London, Wren rebuilt 53 of the 87 churches destroyed. Of these churches nestling close to St Paul's Mackmurdo wrote: 'This united group of church towers, each of which ministers to the other by counterpoint of form, by playing change of outline, and variety of form, Wren was so careful in planning, that no two similar outlines neighbours each other; seldom has he placed together two steeples in equal strength of tone.'

By 1850 only 49 such churches were left. In 1854 the then Bishop of London listed 29 to be demolished because the Church of England could no longer afford to maintain them, *The Times* decrying his plan as 'a vast act of desecration.' 14 churches were destroyed in 1888 and a further eight later on under the Union of Benefices Act. In 1926 19 churches were threatened including Hawksmoor's only City of London church, but eventually, such were the protests that only one was lost. But then the Blitz damaged or destroyed 20 of the remaining 47 churches. Some were restored, but St Andrew-by-the-Wardrobe, St Lawrence Jewry and St Mary-le-Bow have lost their interiors for ever and are thus only Wren churches in name.

The bombing of London caused sorrow in many hearts. The writer, James Pope-Hennessy, who accompanied the photographer, Cecil Beaton, on many tours of bomb-damaged London, as they worked together on a book, *History Under Fire*, was determined to avoid a hostile or sentimental tone. He wrote:

> In the first place it is patent that the bombing of buildings, however ancient and magnificent, cannot be considered as criminal as the bombing of living civilians. In the second place we should admit that certain English buildings, by their proximity to military objectives, must inevitably be destroyed. The London docks, like those of Hamburg, are legitimate objectives; St Paul's Cathedral is not.

The Blitz did as much damage to London's churches as the Dissolution of the Monasteries, the Great Fire of London and the worst efforts of 19th century developers. It destroyed much of medieval London. Nazi bombs destroyed Austin Friars and All-Hallows-by-the-Tower. It destroyed Guildhall. Ten Wren churches, Guildhall, and All-Hallows, Barking were destroyed in one night – 30 December 1940.

London has been redeveloped at alarming speed in the last decades. Not everyone is sympathetic to these changes. As long ago as 1989 in *A Vision of Britain* The Prince of Wales pronounced against the modern buildings that dwarfed Wren's masterpieces, describing the National Theatre as 'a clever way of building a nuclear power station in the middle of London,'. He continued:

> As you continue down the river it is poignant that you can only just glimpse Wren's Monument to the Great Fire as you pass the dreadful Mondial House. To me this building is redolent of a word processor. I don't see that people particularly want a perpetual view of a word processor when they find themselves living with them all the time at the office.

When he wrote *A Vision of Britain*, London Bridge City (where City Hall now stands) was still just an artist's impression. The Prince showed three possibilities – Venetian, Anonymous Modern and Romantic Gothic Revival. He cannot have cared much for the final version.

The original Walkway continued to Tower Bridge and then crossed over to the Tower of London where it ended. But the Western Loop encourages walkers to take the Millennium Bridge, continue up to St Paul's Cathedral and return in the direction of Leicester Square via Ludgate Hill, Fleet Street, Chancery Lane, up to Lincoln's Inn Fields, along Queen Street, down to the Royal Opera House, along Russell Street, past the Transport Museum and finally back to Leicester Square.

Until 2000 the Millennium Bridge was not an option, so it is easier to now follow the Eastern Loop – along to Tower Bridge and finally to the Royal Exchange.

Section 2 – The Eastern Loop

This is a circular walk in the Eastern part of London following the River along the South Bank, crossing Tower Bridge and passing through the City. It rejoins the Thames on the north side of the Millennium Bridge.

Passing Bankside Gallery (home of the Royal Watercolour Society and the Royal Society of Painter Printmakers), Cardinal's Wharf and Provost's Lodge (where Wren lived and where Catherine of Aragon sheltered in 1502), the walker strays into Tudor Britain in the form of the Globe Theatre. This dates back to the 1500s. Shakespeare moved to Southwark in 1599 after he became a shareholder in the theatre. The theatre was burnt down in 1613 during a production of Henry VIII and though rebuilt, was demolished when all places of entertainment were closed down in 1644. Centuries later the actor Sam Wanamaker undertook to rebuild the Globe. His dream was only achieved in 1997 but by then he had been dead for four years. Now the Globe is open for plays and it is possible to tour the theatre during the daytime.

ABOVE The Globe Theatre.

BELOW Sam Wanamaker (second right) with his panel next to Old Thameside Inn on 28 July 1988.

There follow the Financial Times Building, Southwark Bridge, the Clink Prison Museum (telling the history of prisons and explaining the phrase 'in the clink'), Pickford's Wharf and Old Thameside Inn, next to which stands Drake's *Golden Hinde*,

The Walkway on the South Bank with the Clink Prison Museum in the background.

The *Golden Hinde*, a full-sized replica of the ship in which Sir Francis Drake circumnavigated the world.

a full sized model of the ship in which Sir Francis Drake circumnavigated the world between 1577 and 1580.

The Walkway dips inland to incorporate Southwark Cathedral. The former Priory Church of St Marie Overie at Southwark is one of only three churches in London that survive from the great monasteries of London. In the early 19th century it became hemmed in by warehouses and by the railway viaduct to London Bridge, and as a result, somewhat hidden. It was raised to Cathedral status in 1905, and greatly cleaned in 2000.

After Southwark Cathedral, cobbled Montague Close leads round to the right. The Walkway passes

under London Bridge and Montague Close gives way to Tooley Street. Important landmarks before Tower Bridge include Glaziers' Hall and Hay's Galleria. This riverside development was built on the site of Hay's Wharf by St Martin's Property Corporation, a Kuwaiti firm, and opened in 1987. In so doing the riparian route was opened as part of the London Bridge City development.

London Bridge is the latest of several such bridges. Here the Romans bridged the Thames. Then there was a medieval bridge with many arches beneath it and a shopping street across it. The present bridge (built in 1972) is the fourth London Bridge and replaced the bridge which was sold and rebuilt in

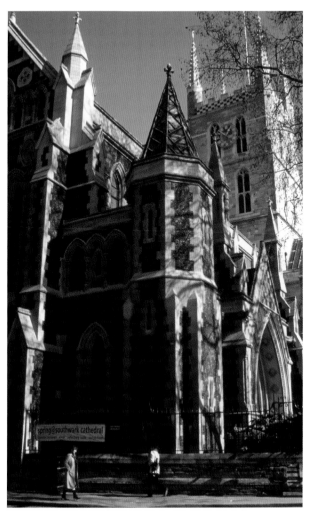

Arizona, USA. (Some say the purchaser thought he was buying Tower Bridge). The steps on the southwest side are known as Nancy's Steps (from Dickens's *Oliver Twist*).

Next comes Southwark Crown Court and then HMS *Belfast*, built in 1938 and then the largest cruiser in the Royal Navy. She served throughout the Second World War taking a leading part in the Battle of the North Cape when the German battle cruiser *Scharnhorst* was sunk. She also took part in the Normandy landings. She was in service until 1965 and since 1971 has been now permanently moored in the Thames as a museum.

This part of The Queen's Walk coincides with the Thames Path National Trail on the south side of the River. This is a trail stretching 294 kilometres from its source in Gloucestershire to the Thames Barrier.

The Walkway leads to City Hall, headquarters of the Mayor of London and of the London Assembly and the GLA (Greater London Authority). It began to operate in 2002. It comprises a meeting chamber, committee rooms, offices and certain public facilities. Fine views of London are afforded from its top floor terraces. It was designed by Foster and Partners, whose brief was to create a building for the GLA

LEFT Southwark Cathedral.

BELOW HMS *Belfast*.

ABOVE Tower Bridge on Diamond Jubilee night, June 5 2012.

ABOVE LEFT City Hall, the home of the London Assembly and Greater London Authority.

BELOW LEFT The Tower of London.

that would become a new landmark for the capital.

Tower Bridge is reached. Now one of London's great landmarks, it was opened as recently as 30 June 1894 by The Prince of Wales (later Edward VII) in the presence of The Princess of Wales (later Queen Alexandra) and The Duke of York (later George V). It is a bascule bridge, designed by Sir John Wolfe Barry, the civil engineer, who also designed the latest version of Greenland Dock. The bridge was originally built to cater for the commercial development taking place in the East End, and had to open to admit tall vessels into the Pool of London. In 1977, to celebrate The Queen's Silver Jubilee, it was painted red and blue.

Crossing Tower Bridge, the Tower of London stands at the point where the Roman city wall reached the Thames, just outside the present City of London. William the Conqueror built the central White Tower to defend the city of London. The Tower is now surrounded by 13th century walls. For five centuries it was a royal palace and has been home to the Royal Mint, the original Royal Observatory, was a celebrated prison and even a zoo (before the exotic animals were transferred to the London Zoo in Regent's Park in the 1830s.

Three Queens were executed on Tower Green – Anne Boleyn and Katherine Howard (wives of Henry VIII) and Lady Jane Grey. It is said that Henry VI was murdered in the Wakefield Tower in 1471 and the two 'Princes in the Tower' (Edward V and his brother, the Duke of York) in the Garden Tower in 1483. When she was a princess, Elizabeth I was held prisoner here for eight weeks in 1554. Eleven spies were shot here during the First World War between 1914 and 1916, including the German spy, Carl Hans Lody, shot there by a firing squad in 1914, and now buried in East London Cemetery. Rudolph Hess was imprisoned here after his dramatic arrival in Scotland in May 1941. On the side of the river is Traitors' Gate, now closed up, through which hapless prisoners would be conveyed inside, seldom to depart alive.

The Crown Jewels are housed in the Tower of London and displayed except when required for a Coronation or State Opening of Parliament.

Here is the St Katharine Docks loop.

St Katharine Docks are to the right of Tower Bridge. This is one of the few surviving docks of London, once nearly concreted over but fortunately saved. Named after the former hospital of St Katharine's by the Tower, the docks were constructed as two linked basins. Opened in 1828, they were eventually merged with the neighbouring London Docks. In

St Katharine Docks.

Royal Exchange was originally built by Sir Thomas Gresham in 1566, though the present building dates from 1844. It is now a shopping and restaurant emporium. At the tip of this triangular island is the statue of the Duke of Wellington, the Iron Duke, on a horse. To the left, in Threadneedle Street, stands the Bank of England, central bank of the United Kingdom. Nearby is Mansion House, home of the Lord Mayor of London who lives and works there during his year of office. Since it was first occupied in 1752 Mansion House has been one of the grandest Georgian town palaces in London.

On a corner to the west stands One Poultry. Outside it is a panoramic panel facing the Bank and Royal Exchange, as well as a gold pavement disc where The Queen stood to unveil this panel which celebrated her Golden Jubilee and a complete refurbishment of the Jubilee Walkway in 2002.

Section 3 of the Walkway starts at this interpretation panel.

The route back to Leicester Square heads down Queen Victoria Street, where there is a link to the left towards Millennium Bridge down Peter's Hill pedestrian area. For Leicester Square, turn right towards St Paul's Cathedral, turn left at the Cathedral and head towards Ludgate Hill.

One of the trees opposite the steps of the Cathedral is a Walkway tree, planted in 2005. The Walkway goes down Ludgate Hill and crosses Farringdon Street into Fleet Street past the former newspaper office buildings (and pubs), past the Law Courts on the right and into the Strand. (There is a panoramic panel outside St Clement Dane's, the RAF church, ahead but not quite on the route). The Walkway turns right into Chancery Lane, passing an information panel outside King's College, which marked the opening of this part of the route by The Duke of Gloucester. Just beyond there is another Walkway tree, planted in 2011.

Section 4 of the Walkway continues north along Chancery Lane.

To regain Leicester Square by the original route, the walker heads left into Carey Street, right into

1909 they were taken over by the Port of London Authority. They were badly damaged by bombs in the war and sold to the GLC in 1968. In the early 1970s they were developed as a marina, with shops and luxury apartments, a highly successful urban development.

The Walkway winds round the dock, passes behind the Tower of London past All-Hallows-by-the-Tower church and through the City of London along Eastcheap and up King William Street to the Royal Exchange.

Along the way is the Monument to the Great Fire of London in 1666, with a 61 metres tall Doric column, designed by Christopher Wren and Robert Hooke and topped with a gilded urn of fire.

When it reaches the Royal Exchange the Walkway is in the heart of the City of London. The majestic

The Law Courts.

The Royal Opera House is one of the finest in the world, often described simply as 'Covent Garden'. This is the home of the Royal Opera and the Royal Ballet. The Walkway now turns into Covent Garden itself, passing the old cast iron floral hall, where the flower market used to be. The London Transport Museum is on the left. The Walkway then passes along cobbled King Street, crosses Bedford Street, goes along New Row, turns into Bedfordbury and into a tiny alleyway called Goodwins Court. This was the one spot on the whole route where it was not possible to make disabled access down into St Martin's Lane.

This is the world of the theatres, swiftly crossed as the Walkway then goes straight ahead into Cecil Court, a pedestrianised area with many second hand bookshops. It takes a left turn in Charing Cross Road which it crosses at the zebra crossing, enters Irving Street (with the National Portrait Gallery on the left) and reaches its starting point in Leicester Square.

Serle Street and crosses into Lincoln's Inn Fields, making a path through the gardens. A feature of the north side of the square is the Sir John Soane Museum at Number 13, containing the collection of John Soane (1753-1837), the son of a bricklayer who became a distinguished architect and designed the Bank of England).

The Walkway continues east across Kingsway into Great Queen Street, winding its way past the Freemasons' Hall to the Royal Opera House in Bow Street.

That was the main route of the original Walkway. Since then there have been three further additions, loops that join the Walkway at various points.

RIGHT Guildhall in the heart of the City of London.

BELOW Lincoln's Inn Fields.

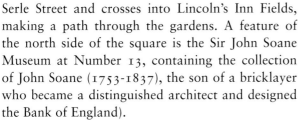

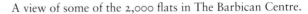
A view of some of the 2,000 flats in The Barbican Centre.

The Walkway leaves the courtyard via an alley marked Guildhall Buildings into Basinghall Street heading north. There is a narrow alley, Mason's Avenue, with pubs and shops. This leads into Coleman Street and heads towards London Wall. The Walkway crosses London Wall in front of Moor House (a curved glass building) and leads over Moor Fields (a pedestrian area) with grass and trees. Just before Moorgate Station it takes a left turn, rising up the escalator to Moorfields Highwalk above the traffic and towards the Barbican Arts Centre.

Here there is a yellow painted line on the ground and the occasional Walkway markers point the way by the crown with additional guidance – signs for the Barbican Centre.

The Barbican was built on the bomb-devastated site of a medieval community which descended into an overcrowded residential area. It contains a housing estate, opened in 1969, and the Barbican Arts Centre, one of the largest performing arts centres in Europe. Here about 4,000 people live in just over 2,000 flats. There are many outdoor areas, water features and benches.

The Walkway passes right through the Barbican and heads south reaching the Museum of London (the world's largest urban history museum) before going down Aldersgate Street, turning right into St Paul's Churchyard, passing the Cathedral to the left and Temple Bar on the right.

Temple Bar was the gateway to the City of London and stood in Fleet Street until 1878. When Fleet Street was widened, it was taken down stone by stone and bought by the brewer, Sir Henry Meux who rebuilt it on land at his home, Theobald's Park in Hertfordshire. It languished there, neglected and in decline until 2003 when (despite a ruling in Sir Henry's will which stated it must never leave Theobald's Park) it was rebuilt opposite St Paul's Cathedral as the gateway into Paternoster Square.

The Walkway rejoins Section 1 and continues down Ludgate Hill.

Section 3 – The City Loop

This is a short circular walk in the City of London that connects the Walkway to the Barbican Centre. It starts at the panoramic panel at One Poultry. Instead of going down Queen Victoria Street, the walker heads up Poultry to Cheapside.

Starting at Number One Poultry, a large dark-pink and white stone building on the corner of Poultry and Queen Victoria Street, the walker takes Poultry which soon becomes Cheapside and turns right into King Street and crosses Gresham Street into Guildhall Yard. Here is Guildhall and the Guildhall Art Gallery, housing a large collection of art relating to London.

Section 4 – The Camden Loop

The entrance to The British Library.

This is a circular walk in the London Borough of Camden connecting the City with the main line stations in the North. This has become more important since it reaches not only St Pancras but Euston Station to which the Eurostar brings visitors from Europe.

This section starts beside the panel on King's College in Chancery Lane and rejoins Section 1 (the Western Loop) at the junction of Kingsway/Great Queen Street.

The Camden Loop heads north up Chancery Lane, crosses Holborn and again heads north to Coram's Fields (named after Captain Thomas Coram who set up the Foundling Hospital in the 18th century) and Brunswick Square. This area is rich with 18th and early 19th century terraces, squares and crescents, many with fine wrought iron balconies and railings. Much of this land was owned by the Dukes of Bedford, hence names such as Russell and Woburn.

The Walkway passes Brunswick Square Gardens and the modern Brunswick Centre, leading north by a circuitous largely residential route to Euston Road where King's Cross Station (newly revamped for the Olympics in 2012) is to the right.

The Walkway itself turns left on Euston Road past St Pancras Station and the tall spires of the 19th century St Pancras Hotel and past the British Library which moved there from the British Museum in 1998 and holds over 13 million books, along with journals, manuscripts, maps, printed music and sound recordings.

The Walkway takes a dip down into Judd Street and Hastings Street into Cartwright Gardens, a crescent of town houses. It turns right into Burton Place, right again at Burton Street, and then follows

Carlton House Terrace from the Mall.

This is a circular walk up the Mall to Buckingham Palace and down Birdcage Walk, rejoining the original Walkway at Great Queen Street.

This route was created in 2003 to celebrate The Queen's Golden Jubilee the previous year and to recognise that millions of people gathered in the Mall to cheer The Queen on 4 June 2002. It starts opposite the Duke of York Steps and the route up the Mall is marked uniquely with gold discs.

On the north side is the fine façade of Carlton House Terrace next to the Duke of York steps, with its large pink granite column and bronze statue of 'the Grand Old Duke of York', Commander-in-chief of the British Army during the French Revolutionary Wars who led his men to the top of the hill and led them back again. The Duke was the second son of King George III. The column was designed by Sir Richard Westmacott in 1834.

The Mall is boarded by St James's Park (the oldest Royal Park in London) on the left. On the right there is much to see and this and an alternative view are depicted on a double-sided panel on that side of the Mall. After Carlton House Terrace comes Carlton Gardens, No 1 being by tradition the home of the Foreign Secretary. Jeffrey Sterling ran the London Celebrations Committee from his office at 4 Carlton Gardens, the erstwhile wartime office of General de Gaulle. The Queen Mother unveiled a statue to the General in the square in 1993 and facing the Mall are the statues of King George VI by Sir William Reid Dick and of the Queen Mother by Philip Jackson. Both are depicted wearing the robes of the Order of the Garter.

Beyond is Marlborough House, now the headquarters of the Commonwealth Secretariat. It was originally built for Sarah, Duchess of Marlborough by Sir Christopher Wren in 1711. It was the London home of Edward VII and Queen Alexandra as Prince and Princess of Wales from 1863 until 1901, and then of the next Prince and Princess of Wales (the future George V and Queen Mary) until 1910. Queen Alexandra then used it in widowhood until her death in 1925, as did Queen Mary between 1936 and her death in 1953.

the cobbled Dukes Road into Woburn Walk. Then it goes north again up Upper Woburn Place and left onto Euston Road, passing Euston Station behind Euston Square Gardens.

After this it turns south down Gordon Street, past University College London, to Gordon Square with its central park and down to Russell Square via the campus of the School for Oriental Studies.

The last part of the loop goes right through the middle of the British Museum. This famous museum owes its origins to the will of Sir Hans Sloane (1660-1753), the physician, naturalist and collector who wanted his collection of over 71,000 objects, library and herbarium to be preserved intact after his death. It opened in 1759 and now attracts more than 5 million visitors a year.

The Walkway then goes into Great Russell Street, down Museum Street, with its pavement cafés, along Bloomsbury Way and into Sicilian Avenue, an Italianate pedestrian area completed in 1910 with columns at the entrance. The Walkway then goes south down Southampton Row, crosses High Holborn and rejoins Section 1 at the junction with Great Queen Street and Remnant Street.

Section 1 of the Walkway heads right along Great Queen Street.

On the other side of Marlborough Road stands St James's Palace, one of London's oldest palaces, originally commissioned by Henry VIII. The first three King Georges lived there before George III took over Buckingham Palace, which Queen Victoria turned into the official residence of the Sovereign in 1837. Since then St James's Palace has remained the official Court to which ambassadors are accredited. The new Sovereign attends the Accession Council there. It is used for many receptions and over the years members of the Royal Family have had apartments there.

Clarence House adjoins St James's Palace and they share a garden. It was built by John Nash between 1825 and 1827 for the Duke of Clarence (later William IV). Since then its royal occupants have included his sister, Princess Augusta; the Duchess of Kent (mother of Queen Victoria); Prince Alfred, Duke of Edinburgh, and Prince Arthur, Duke of Connaught (sons of Queen Victoria). The present Queen lived there following her marriage until 1952, and from 1953 until 2002 it was the home of Queen Elizabeth The Queen Mother. After her death The Prince of Wales moved in and he now lives there with his second wife, The Duchess of Cornwall.

Lancaster House is the other large house on the right hand side of the Mall. It was designed in 1825 by Benjamin Deane Wyatt for the Duke of York and Albany but was still largely unfinished when the Duke died in 1827. It was then bought by the 2nd Marquess of Stafford (later 1st Duke of Sutherland) and called Stafford House for nearly a century. In 1912 it was bought by 1st Viscount Leverhulme who presented it to the nation in 1924. It is now used for government hospitality and is where Commonwealth Conferences and G8 summits are held if they are in London.

At the end of the Mall stands Buckingham Palace which has served as the official London residence of Britain's sovereigns since 1837. It was originally a town house owned in the 18th century by the Dukes of Buckingham. Now it is The Queen's official residence with State Apartments for entertaining and comprises her London office. It is the focal point to which the people of Britain turn on great national occasions. The Queen and her family come out onto the balcony and crowds frequently stretch well into the Mall. When The Queen is away in the summer, the Palace is open to visitors.

In front of Buckingham Palace is the Queen Victoria Memorial, a white marble column with a statue of Queen Victoria facing The Mall, completed in 1911. These views are interpreted on a panoramic panel, unveiled opposite the Palace to mark the

Buckingham Palace.

79

Golden Wedding of The Queen and The Duke of Edinburgh, celebrated in November 1997.

Buckingham Palace was again the focus of national attention during the Diamond Jubilee celebrations, with a picnic in the Palace grounds, a pop concert around the Victoria Memorial, and the next day a balcony appearance by The Queen and her immediate heirs, with a fly-past to round off the day.

The Walkway then turns round the western edge of St James's Park and back down Birdcage Walk, again on the edge of the park. It passes Wellington Barracks, where the Footguards are stationed when on duty, and the Guards Chapel, originally built in 1838 as the regimental chapel of the Brigade of Guards, but rebuilt in 1960 after it was bombed by a V1 during Sunday matins on 18 June 1944, with 121 killed and 141 injured.

At the end of Birdcage Walk the Walkway leads into Great George Street, linking to Section 1.

* * * * *

The Walkway gives many the chance to get to know different aspects of London in its ever-changing process of development. There is ceremonial London, royal London, there is the seat of government and the great Abbey where the Kings and Queens of Britain are crowned. Across the Thames The Queen's Walk has opened up the riparian route and millions now use that as a way to walk to work.

These various areas have their own atmosphere, evoking reminders of Tudor Britain, Dickensian London and views to the surviving Wren churches gamely holding their own against the intrusion of the vast new glass office buildings and skyscrapers that are a feature of commercial London. The Walkway goes through the city and links that to the West End with its opera house and its theatres. There are residential areas and there are open spaces. There are wide avenues and intimate pedestrian passages. There are loops that explore St Katharine Docks, the Barbican, the City and Camden. In fact there is something for everybody.

For those who want to explore different areas of the great city of London and to see how it works and fits together, this is the route to follow.

The Jubilee Walkway can help people fully understand London. The Trust has delivered and enhanced Max Nicholson's original vision of a silver thread linking the West End, the South Bank, East London and the City. To the work of Robert Shaw and the early Trustees The Queen paid tribute in a speech in 1994: 'Though I can't guarantee that I shall walk every step of it myself in the years to come, I know that those who do, tired though they may be at the end, will share my gratitude and pleasure at a job that has been well and truly done.'

St James's Park in springtime.

Route of the Jubilee Greenway

The Jubilee Greenway complements the Walkway and in some parts the two routes overlap, notably on the South Bank. The route extends 60 kilometres round London – one for each year of The Queen's reign. It is marked by some 500 discs, made of reconstituted glass, decorated in green with the Gothic crown, two diamonds on either side and laurel wreaths.

The route's logical beginning is at Buckingham Palace and here The Queen opened it on 29 February 2012. It travels up Constitution Hill, through Hyde Park to the Broad Walk in Kensington Gardens, along the Bayswater Road to Paddington and the Pool of Little Venice, then along the Regent's Canal to Victoria Park, through the main Olympic site at Stratford, along the Greenway and down to the Thames through Beckton District Park, then over (or under) the river to Woolwich and back along the Thames Path to the Tower of London and The Queen's Walk where it rejoins the Jubilee Walkway eventually returning to Buckingham Palace.

The Greenway is divided into 12 sections:

Section 1 – Buckingham Palace to Queensway

The Jubilee Greenway starts at Buckingham Palace, the London residence of Her Majesty The Queen and the focal point for national celebrations. On such occasions, great television studios are built by Canada Gate to house the world's media and behind them stretches an entire media village. Throughout the year, almost daily, there is the Changing of the Guard, while behind the great façade of the Palace, The Queen deals with affairs of state, receiving the Prime Minister, investing worthy citizens, entertaining Heads of State from other lands, and giving garden parties on the lawns behind.

The route passes up Constitution Hill, leaving the Palace on the left, goes through the Memorial Gates (opened by The Queen in November 2002 as a memorial to the five million volunteers from the Commonwealth who died in the Second World War),

and heads towards Hyde Park. It passes Wellington Arch (originally designed to be a magnificent gateway to Buckingham Palace, in the reign of George IV) and then enters Hyde Park through the gates known as the Hyde Park Corner Screen.

The first part of the route is adjacent to Green Park and nearby are a number of war memorials at Hyde Park Corner and the famous 'Number One London' – Apsley House, London home of the Dukes of Wellington.

Hyde Park is the most famous of the Royal Parks, described by William Pitt the Elder as 'the lung of London'. It contains the Serpentine – 28 acres of water created in 1730 on the instructions of Queen Caroline (wife of George II), and crossed by a stone bridge.

ABOVE Wellington Arch, Hyde Park Corner.

ABOVE RIGHT The Commonwealth Memorial on Constitution Hill.

RIGHT The Royal Albert Hall.

The Greenway passes along South Carriage Drive or Rotten Row (where the Household Cavalry can sometimes been seen exercising) and reaches Kensington Gardens, first created by Queen Anne and landscaped by Queen Caroline in 1733. Nearby are Knightsbridge Barracks, the Royal Albert Hall (opened by Queen Victoria in 1871), and the Albert Memorial – the national memorial to her husband, the Prince Consort, directly to its north. The Albert Memorial was commissioned by Queen Victoria and

Queen Victoria's statue by her daughter, Princess Louise, Duchess of Argyll, outside Kensington Palace.

designed by Sir George Gilbert Scott as the foremost of many memorials to the Prince, who died in 1861. In fact his will stated that he wished there to be no memorials to him of any kind.

The route then turns right onto the Broad Walk past Kensington Palace, where William III settled in 1689, where Queen Victoria was born in 1819 and Queen Mary (future wife of George V) in 1867 and where to this day members of the Royal Family live. The entrance to the Palace has lately been given an ambitious makeover to encourage visitors to come and see the State Apartments and the collections of historic royal costumes. More prominent now is the statue of Queen Victoria, by her daughter, Princess Louise, Duchess of Argyll, herself a long time resident of Kensington Palace.

On the other side is Round Pond (in fact more oval than circular) with extensive views over the park. The route continues through Black Lion Gate, crosses the road and turns right along Bayswater Road.

Section 2 – Queensway to Paddington

Royal London is left behind and the route makes its way along the busy highway of the Bayswater Road, which then gives way to the more residential area of Bayswater, the scene gradually changing once more to something more hectic as Bayswater is succeeded by Paddington. Private houses, some fine, some less so, vie with restaurants and shops

The Diana, Princess of Wales memorial in Hyde Park.

and all around are hotels to accommodate the many travellers who arrive at Paddington Station or stay in the area before their journeys.

The Greenway diverts through Craven Hill Gardens, one of the least likely streets to find itself part of such a route, but it leads into Craven Hill, Praed Street and the bustle of Paddington. From a sightseeing point of view this is not the most visually stimulating part of the route. The buildings have been converted to contain perhaps too many apartments, but there are some attractive mewses and a host of restaurants.

Paddington used to be part of Middlesex. In 1815 it was but a small hamlet, the area adjoining its canals being basically rural. This changed when Isambard Kingdom Brunel and Matthew Digby Wyatt built the main line railway station there in 1847. Great shops such as Whiteley's sprung up in 1911. An area which had been farmland was gradually converted towards urban housing, much of the construction

ABOVE The Serpentine.

BELOW Sheldon Square, Paddington.

The Pool of Little Venice, with Browning's Island in the background.

work taking place in the 1840s and 1850s.

Every day commuters arrive at Paddington Station from places such as Slough, Maidenhead, Reading and Swindon, and the service extends as far as South Wales and Cornwall. The Heathrow Express is now a popular route to Heathrow Airport, taking passengers there in 15 minutes.

Section 3 – Paddington to Little Venice

This Section leads from the buzz of Paddington to the Pool of Little Venice, the basin of the Regent's Canal, and thus through several changes of atmosphere, into an especially appealing route for walkers and cyclists. This part has changed a lot in the past few years and continues to develop at great pace.

After Paddington Station, a sharp left turn leads into South Wharf Road, past St Mary's Hospital,

Paddington (birthplace of The Duke of Cambridge in 1982 and Prince Harry in 1984). A good view of Paddington Basin (terminus of the Paddington Arm of the Grand Union Canal, opened in 1801) can be had by making a short detour to the right. Then a narrow pedestrian way leads towards Sheldon Square. Travellers pour out of the station on the left, there are smart restaurants and presently the Grand Union Canal (Paddington Branch) borders the route to its right. This emerges at the Pool of Little Venice.

Browning's Island, where Canada Geese and swans congregate in some seasons, hoves into view. To the left is Warwick Crescent where the poet, Robert Browning lived. Ahead the canal heads towards Camden, Victoria Park and down to Limehouse Basin and the Thames. Walkers and cyclists follow the north bank of the canal.

Little Venice has only been so named since the 1850s. It was originally known as Paddington but transformed into a busy transport route when the Regent's Canal arrived in 1801. It is sometimes said that Browning first called it Little Venice. In

ABOVE Blomfield Road, Little Venice.

RIGHT An aptly named long boat in the Pool of Little Venice.

fact Lord Byron coined the name, comparing this area of Paddington unfavourably to Venice in Italy. Byron thought the waterways as potentially fine as the canals of Venice but let down by the shabby, run-down housing around them. He wrote: 'There would be nothing to make the canal of Venice more poetical than that of Paddington, were it not for its artificial adjuncts.'

The fine houses in Blomfield Road were built in Victorian times, their designs inspired by the Nash houses of Regent's Park. Some survive, but many have been replaced by apartment buildings. The area was always noted for the sharp contrast between the smart houses of the Victorian gentry and the canal boats of the boatmen and their families who lived and worked on the canal.

Section 4 – Little Venice to Camden

This Section runs along the Regent's Canal, past Regent's Park and the London Zoo, through a variety of areas – residential, business and recreational, and finally to Camden. This is one of the most soothing and attractive parts of the Greenway, packed with interest, changing tone and atmosphere from one bridge to the next, from the quiet of Little Venice to the hotbed atmosphere of Camden Lock Market. There are two places where there is no towpath and it is necessary to cross overland before once again walking along the canalside.

Waterbuses pass through the long Maida Hill Tunnel but pedestrians and cyclists follow the towpath on the north side of the canal, later taking the slight incline of Blomfield Road leading to Maida Vale on the left and Edgware Road on the right. They eventually rejoin the towpath after Lisson Grove. They begin on the south side of the canal but presently cross to the north side over a small pedestrian bridge. After that the towpath is followed all the way to Camden with only one left turn under Prince Albert Road Bridge.

The Regent's Canal (named after the Prince Regent, the future George IV) passes under many bridges, none so dramatic as Macclesfield Bridge, originally called North Gate Bridge, being the northern carriage entrance to Regent's Park. It is colloquially known as 'Blow-Up Bridge', because in October 1874 it was blown up when a barge carrying gunpowder exploded, the explosion being heard twenty miles away. Canal men were killed and the villa of the famous Anglo-Dutch artist, Sir Lawrence Alma-Tadema, on the north side of the park and his collection of classical art was destroyed in the blast. Most of the bridge itself was also destroyed but the cast-iron columns were re-used when the bridge was rebuilt.

The area soon becomes better kept, especially when it reaches the beautifully manicured lawns and fine houses to the north of Regent's Park. This is one of the most beautiful stretches of waterway in England. Here are handsome villas built in the 1980s and 1990s to original Nash designs. On the north side is a house dating back to 1730, owned by the Nuffield Foundation. Passing under various bridges, the Snowdon Aviary on the left (part of London Zoo, designed by the Earl of Snowdon, Cedric Price and Frank Newby, and opened in 1965) is to the left.

Regent's Park, again named after George IV and first opened to the public in 1845, is a 487-acre park, landscaped by John Nash and completed in 1838 on the south side of the canal. It is one of the Royal Parks with a fine lake, an area containing London Zoo. There is Queen Mary's Rose Garden and the Open Air Theatre, opened in 1932, the oldest permanent outdoor theatre in Britain.

London Zoo was originally opened in 1828 as a collection for scientific study, and to the general public in 1847. It serves as a home for a wide variety of animals (over 755 species) and is the international headquarters for research and conservation work of the Zoological Society.

Cumberland Basin is next with the romantic red building of the Feng Shang Princess Floating Chinese Restaurant to the fore. This was a branch of the Regent's Canal leading to an earlier Cumberland Basin, but it was disused by 1937 and filled in with rubble from bomb damage after the war.

Here is the sharp left turn under Prince Albert Road Bridge. Presently the Pirate Castle, headquarters of the Pirate Club is in view. A little further on this section ends at Camden Lock and Camden Market.

The Regent's Canal was originally built as a link between the Paddington arm of the Grand Junction Canal, opened in 1801, with the Thames at Limehouse. Seaborne cargo arrived at Regent's Canal Docks at Limehouse and was offloaded onto canal barges, which were then pulled by horses to their destinations. Along the towpath there are still marks on the bridges where the ropes ate into the ironwork, some of the bridges have black and white bars to prevent this from happening. Sometimes the barges passed under tunnels, at which point the horses ceased to pull them, and men lay on top of the barges and pushed the boats along with their feet on the roof of the tunnels. This process was called 'legging'.

John Nash designed the canal which was completed in two stages – Paddington to Camden in 1816 and the rest to Limehouse in 1820. Its excavation was not without problems. The budget over-ran, a hydro-pneumatic lock at Hampstead Road failed to work and one of the promoters of the lock embezzled some funds. Getting the water in presented another problem. The River Brent was dammed to create a reservoir and various basins were excavated. The canal has a number of locks along its way since the height rises some

ABOVE A Jubilee Greenway disc being inserted into the path of the Regent's Canal.

ABOVE RIGHT Macclesfield Bridge (or 'Blow-up Bridge').

CENTRE RIGHT The Snowdon Aviary at London Zoo.

BELOW RIGHT The Feng Shang Princess Floating Chinese Restaurant on the Regent's Canal.

86 metres from the Thames to Little Venice. In the end the canal cost £772,000, twice the estimate. Nevertheless, the canal did open in 1820 and soon became an important means of transporting freight.

The canal is no longer used for moving goods (though Tesco still bring its wines along it to this day). In 1953 small motor tractors were introduced to pull the barges and the last commercial horse-drawn barge ceased to work in 1956. By the late 1960s, with the opening of sections of the towpath to the general public by Westminster in 1968 and Camden in 1974, it took on a new role as a leisure facility.

Some of the basins have been filled in – notably at Limehouse and City Road, a smaller access being

formed between the canal and the Thames. Boats ply their way between Little Venice and Camden with tourists on board and there are a number of residential houseboats on certain stretches of the canal, notably near Little Venice.

This section ends at Camden Lock. In the 19th century this was but one of many locks on the canal. The lock itself was (and still is) called Hampstead Road Lock – the ill-fated one which had failed to work. The lock is still used today and those that steer the barges open and close the gates themselves.

Near to the lock stood warehouses and other buildings and from 1854 there were stables for the horses that pulled the barges along the canal, and a horse hospital. As canal trade had effectively ceased by 1970, so Camden Lock Market began to appear. This new market started while unsuccessful negotiations to build an urban motorway across the

LEFT AND BELOW Camden Market and Hampstead Road Lock.

site dragged on until 1976. Meanwhile no building was possible. Market stalls sprang up, specialising in clothes and crafts and it soon became immensely popular. Gradually the market expanded and there is now an indoor market hall. The former historic stables were turned into Stables Market, with stallholders setting up in the numerous old horse stables themselves. A wide and delicious variety of ethnic food is also on sale.

Section 5 – Camden to Victoria Park

This Section continues along the Regent's Canal from Camden Lock to Victoria Park – there being a point at Islington where the walker cannot follow the towpath and must again go overland for a while. It passes through Camden, Islington, Hackney and Bethnal Green, leading to Victoria Park. Here can be seen the many ways in which London is developing. There are numerous new constructions, particularly along the south side of the canal.

A number of bridges and locks are passed – including Kentish Town Bridge Road, Camden Street Bridge, Camden Road Bridge, and Royal College Street Bridge, after which there is a sudden view of the Post Office Tower to the right. After the substantial rail bridge serving St Pancras Station, the canal widens into the St Pancras Yacht Basin and St Pancras Lock.

The Islington Tunnel is the longest tunnel of the canal, being 886 metres long. It was opened in 1820. Once legging proved tiring, a steamboat tug was introduced to pull the barges through it. The tunnel

ABOVE AND BELOW Two views along the Regent's Canal near Camden Lock.

is especially straight. As there is no towpath, the Greenway route goes overland through a housing estate to Chapel Market in Islington, with numerous street market stalls. It is one of London's liveliest markets and boasts one of the few surviving pie and mash shops in London.

Also overland is Camden Passage, an attractive Georgian street next to Upper Street in Islington, built in about 1776. It now houses the famous antique market with some 350 antique dealers trading there. The tranquillity of the towpath is now superseded by the full onslaught of traffic which is Upper Street. Camden Passage, the well-known antique market, is close by and presently an unmarked wall with a wrought iron gate leads down a steep hill and back to the towpath.

Along this route are some notable landmarks – Camley Street Natural Park, a 2-acre nature reserve, St Pancras Yacht Basin and St Pancras Waterpoint (a 350-ton listed Gothic-style water tank built in

ABOVE A Georgian house on the Regent's Canal.

BELOW The Regent's Canal as it skirts Victoria Park.

1872 by Sir George Gilbert Scott to service steam locomotives). The London Canal Museum is the only museum in London that tells the story of inland waterways. It is housed in a former ice warehouse built in 1862/3 for Carlo Gatti, overlooking Battlebridge Basin.

Nearby are King's Cross Station and St Pancras and the Eurostar Terminus, moved there from Waterloo Station in 2007. The canal continues to wind through different moods of London. Not far to its north is Broadway Market, one of London's oldest chartered markets with the atmosphere of a village. At one time a desolate street, it became a thriving market with numerous good restaurants, even a traditional eel pie restaurant, a farmer's market, galleries and shops selling arts and crafts. It is said to have been the inspiration for the popular BBC television series, *EastEnders*, first broadcast in 1985.

This section ends at Victoria Park, which extends to some 218 acres in Tower Hamlets. Here the Regent's Canal joins the Hertford Union Canal, running round the southern perimeter of Victoria Park. It also runs down the Mile End extension to Limehouse, joining the Thames at the Limehouse Basin.

Originally laid out by Sir James Pennethorne between 1842 and 1846, Victoria Park came into being following a petition to Queen Victoria from 30,000 local residents, complaining about the mortality rate in the East End. The population had doubled and fields, market gardens and orchards had disappeared in the cause of urbanisation.

The people of the East End asked for a Royal Park to be created in the Queen's name – 'a Monument to future generations; of your Majesty's taste and patronage of Public improvements; and still more, of the anxious desire of your Majesty to contribute to the happiness of your loyal and devoted subjects.' The petition further stated: 'A Park in the East End of London would probably diminish the annual deaths by several thousands . . . and add several years to the lives of the entire population.' Sir James Pennethorne had been a pupil of the architect, John Nash, and was himself Architect to the Commissioners of Woods and Forests. Thus Victoria Park's design was much inspired by Nash's work in Regent's Park.

ABOVE Broadway Market.

BELOW Bonner Gates at Victoria Park.

Amongst the fine features of 'Vicky Park' as it is sometimes known, are the Bonner Gates and Bridge (built in 1840) at the main entrance to the park, and named after Bishop Edmund Bonner, last Lord of the Manor of Stepney. These fine old gates have not been restored or changed and are as Queen Victoria would have seen them on her only ever visit in 1873.

Just inside these gates, sitting on plinths, are the Dogs of Alcibiades, copies of ancient Greek statuary,

Victoria Park, with a statue of one of the Dogs of
Alcibiades.

given to Victoria Park by Lady Regnart, the widow of Sir Horace Regnart, President of Maple & Co, after his death in 1912.

Queen Victoria did not visit the park that bears her name until 2 April 1873. Lord George Hamilton, MP for Middlesex, who ran the Victoria Park Preservation Society, had long wanted her to come but at first this was not possible. Suddenly, with but 48 hours notice, the visit was announced. Immediately all the areas east of Islington, leading to the Park, put out coloured bunting to adorn shop windows.

Queen Victoria left Buckingham Palace at 10.40 in her carriage, preceded by a few mounted policemen. The procession arrived via Essex Road to the entrance at St Agnes Terrace at the northwest side of the park. Here she received a loyal address, all three local parishes vying with each other not to be upstaged. She made a circuit of the park, led by an escort of the 1st Life Guards. She left by the Bonner Gates and the Approach Road, travelled through the City of London and was back at Buckingham Palace in time for lunch. *The Times* described the visit:

Nothing could have been better than the conduct of the police, but certainly no people could have behaved in a more orderly and creditable manner than the vast mass of those who turned out to see and cheer the Sovereign. Immense numbers were in the park, and the spectators outside the railings were quite as numerous. All the way round omnibuses, waggons and lighter vehicles were drawn up and converted into platforms every foot of which was covered with spectators.

The *Times* correspondent clearly relished the visit, but was less impressed by the park itself:

There are pretty spots in Victoria Park. Here and there art and gardening had done much for it; but whatever it may be in a future day, Victoria Park as seen as a whole from the road around its outer edge is not very attractive.

Queen Victoria sent a reply to the loyal address, in which she said: 'I have long desired to visit this beautiful Park, which supplies the means of healthy and pleasant recreation to the vast population which surrounds it.' She was pleased that they had referred to the interest taken to ameliorate the life and circumstances of the poor by the late Prince Consort, and reaffirmed that 'the health, the enjoyment and the homes of the poorer classes' of her people were 'an interest which I heartily shared with him and which has never ceased to occupy a foremost place in my thoughts.'

Queen Victoria herself considered her visit to what she called 'The Peoples' Park' as 'a splendid day.'

Section 6 – Victoria Park to Greenway

This Section leads from Victoria Park through the main Olympic Site at Stratford and along the route created above the main sewerage system of London, called 'the Greenway'. The route leaves the park via St Mark's Gate and after passing under the A102M, heads up the hill and enters the Greenway itself.

The highlight of this section is the Olympic Park, the focal point of the London 2012 Games. Situated in the Lower Lea Valley, work began in May 2008 with the construction of the Olympic Stadium. The whole site was completed a year ahead of the Games and well within budget.

The Olympic Park was planned to accommodate up to 180,000 spectators a day. The main venues are the Olympic Stadium, Aquatics Centre, Velodrome and the BMX Circuit. There are arena for hockey, handball and basketball. All this is accessed from a central unifying concourse, crossing roads, waterways and rail lines.

The Olympic Village can house thousands of athletes and officials. There is an Olympic Park Loop Road, connecting the Olympic Village to all the venues, and an International Broadcast Centre and Main Press Centre.

As soon as the Games and Para-Olympic Games are over, the area will be transformed into the largest urban park created in Europe for over 150 years. This will restore wetland habitats, involve the canals and waterways of the River Lea being cleaned and widened, and the natural river system of the valley restored. The park will be planted with native species of trees, to provide a home for wildlife in the middle of the city. The Olympic sports facilities will be adapted for use by sports clubs and the local

community and the Olympic Village converted into homes.

9,000 new homes have been built in the park, along with shops, restaurants and cafes. There is an extension to the Docklands Light Railway, increased capacity on the Jubilee Line and Stratford Regional Station has been upgraded. Access to the park has been greatly improved via a network of canal towpaths, footpaths and cycleways.

Stratford International Station connects Stratford City to St Pancras and the rest of Europe, via the Channel Tunnel Rail Link, and is also linked via Crossrail and the Jubilee Line to the rest of London.

The Olympic Park becomes the Queen Elizabeth

The entrance to Bazalgette's Greenway.

Olympic Park in May 2013. Anyone entering the park from the Greenway will cross the major celebratory feature of the Jubilee Greenway – sixty lit discs organised in the style of E II R surmounted by a crown. This magnificent feature was placed there early in February 2012. It unites the Olympic Games with the Diamond Jubilee, both such features of 2012.

The Greenway – as this part of the route is officially known (not to be confused with the Jubilee Greenway) owes its existence to an outbreak of cholera and 'the Great Stink' of 1858. It is a footpath and cycling path that runs from Bow at Wick Lane, through Stratford (the Olympic site), Plaistow and Newham to Royal Docks Road in Beckton.

Originally known as Sewerbank, it runs along the embankment created by the construction of the Northern Outfall Sewer. It was renovated in the mid-1990s and much of it was tidied up in advance of the Olympic Games since it provides pedestrian and cycling access to the great site.

Under the Greenway is the Northern Outfall Sewer designed by Joseph Bazalgette. Originally Londoners depended on some 200,000 cesspits for household waste, which were emptied infrequently. In 1815 permission was granted for household waste to be carried to the River Thames by sewers, an unsatisfactory arrangement. When flush toilets were introduced, replacing chamber pots, the increase in waste in the cesspits greatly increased. These frequently overflowed into street drains which had only been designed to take rainwater. This was unhealthy and in 1853 there was a serious outbreak of cholera in London. Five years later, in 1858, London endured a particularly hot summer, encouraging bacteria to thrive. 'The Great Stink' was so disgusting that it even affected the work of the House of Commons. A select committee was formed to address the issue.

The Metropolitan Board of Works was formed and in 1859 their chief engineer, Joseph Bazalgette,

Abbey Mills Pumping Station.

This Section is a short route that leads from the Greenway down to the Thames at North Woolwich – to the Woolwich Free Ferry above the river and a pedestrian subway below it. As sometimes happens, the route makes its way through alleys and areas of housing, crossing a bridge over the busy thoroughfare of Newham Way (A13) and on through North Beckton into Viking Gardens and Beckton District Park.

The park is bordered by Stansfeld Road on the south, and Tollgate Road on the north. It is an expanse of greenery tucked away in East London. The main path leads through woodland before opening into a meadow that blooms with wild flowers in the spring. Its prime attraction is its large lake with a shingle beach leading to its waters. A tree trail was created to celebrate the Millennium and there is a fishing club, football pitch, nature area, play area, cycle route and basketball court.

A short detour to the right leads to Stansfeld Road, on the other side of which is King George V Park in West Beckton, which contains Newham City Farm. This urban farm was opened in Silver Jubilee year, 1977, as an initiative of the Environmental

Ponies in Beckton District Park.

produced a scheme to take the waste to a treatment plant in Beckton (a large area beyond Docks Road, bordered on the north side by the A13, on the east by Barking Creek and on the south by the Thames).

The Greenway continues with distant views of the great office blocks at Canary Wharf on the Isle of Dogs. A pedestrian may well be reminded from time to time that the sewers are beneath due to occasional whiffs that assault the nostrils. On the right is Abbey Mills Pumping Station, in Abbey Lane, E15, also designed by Joseph Bazalgette. Described as 'the Cathedral of Sewage', it was built in the Byzantine style in the shape of a cruciform. Originally run by steam, it had two huge Moorish-style chimneys which were demolished in the Second World War for fear of being too easily identifiable as targets by German bombers.

The Greenway passes the East London Cemetery, 33 acres at Plaistow, Newham General Hospital (a nucleus hospital opened in 1983), and Brampton Park on Masterman Road, at East Ham, which contains Brampton Primary School, the East Ham Synagogue, and the Jewish Cemetery.

A great number of small roads are crossed until Capital Ring signs direct pedestrians and cyclists to take a right turn through double gates (two metal banners) and down either by steps or a cycle ramp. An alleyway leads between houses, and in due course the Greenway route makes its way towards Beckton District Park.

The Royal Albert Dock Basin.

Committee of the London Celebrations Committee of The Queen's Silver Jubilee, on some disused land at Beckton, formerly playing fields. Beckton District Park gives way to a roadway left of New Beckton Park with a cricket pitch, football pitch, bowling green, games court, play area and tennis court.

Again a housing area has to be navigated. The route here is complicated but eventually leads towards the University of East London Docklands Campus and past the busy Royal Albert Way, both to the right. In due course the Sir Steven Redgrave Bridge (also known as Woolwich Manor Way, renamed after the oarsman who won five Olympic gold medals) is reached. This crosses the Royal Albert Dock Basin. On the left is the large Royal Quay development and later Galleons Point Marina, and on the right Royal Albert Dock and King George V Dock on the right (beyond which is London City Airport). There are distant views of the Dome and Canary Wharf.

This area was famed for its docks. The Royal

Albert Dock was one of the Royal Docks (the largest area of enclosed docks in the world), opened in 1880. The site was 87 acres, the largest purpose built dock in Britain, and was originally planned as an extension of the Royal Victoria Dock (opened by Prince Albert in 1855) to cater for the meat and tobacco trade. The dock was closed to shipping in 1981.

Since then London City Airport (serving many Northern European destinations) has been built on a disused quay between King George V Dock and Royal Albert Dock and opened by The Queen in 1987. In 1997 the Royal Business Park (a development for 1,000 offices) was opened on the north side of the dock, and in 1998 the University of East London opened its Dockland campus at the eastern end of the north quayside. In 2000 Docklands Regatta Centre, a major rowing club, was officially opened.

Canary Wharf from the River Thames.

The dock is now mainly used for water sports and as a rowing course.

Galleons Point Marina, at Royal Albert Basin, is a starting point for cruising by both beginners and experienced yachtsmen which can take vessels up to 72 feet long. The marina used to be the holding area for ships awaiting their unloading berth in Royal Albert Dock.

King George V Dock was another of the Royal Docks. Building began in 1912 but ceased on the outbreak of the First World War, so construction was not completed until 1921. The dock was the last of London's enclosed docks. It could accommodate the largest ships, including liners such as *Mauretania*. At the western end was a large graving dock (since filled in) and a machine shop used for ship repairs by Harland and Wolff. The dock closed to shipping in 1981.

Presently the first view of the Thames comes into view on the left. The Thames is reached at Hobart Wharf, with a view of Woolwich on the other side of the river. The riverside walk leads through Royal Victoria Gardens, which were largely marshlands until 1847, then pleasure gardens attracting large numbers of visitors who had come to London to see the Great Exhibition. Later they became heavily polluted, and by 1884 were notorious as the haunt of prostitutes. The gardens suffered bomb damage in the Second World War. In 1971 they became the responsibility of Newham Council. They were restored by the London Development Agency in 2000.

Nearby is the Old Station Museum, North Woolwich (opened in 1984), a museum containing carriages, locomotives, and other exhibits relating to the railways and local history.

The route finally zigzags its way to the Woolwich Free Ferry (open since 1889) at North Woolwich Pier, which conveys passengers and vehicles across to the south bank of the Thames at Woolwich. Here there is an alternative crossing via the round-domed building – the entrance to the Woolwich Foot Tunnel beneath the Thames.

In ancient times there was a ferry from North

Woolwich to Warren Lane. Various other ferries were built over the years. A steam ferry was suggested as early as 1850, but not until 1880 was the idea made public that such a ferry should be established from local resources. The Metropolitan Board was asked to provide this to offset the cost of bridges built and maintained in the West End of London. The Free Ferry was opened in 1889.

In 1922 the original boats were replaced and in 1930 two new boats were commissioned. In turn these were replaced by three new diesel boats in 1963. Thus the Woolwich Free Ferry has been plying its way between North Woolwich and Woolwich since 1889. There are normally two ferryboats in commission at any time and they convey motor vehicles, cyclists and pedestrians across the Thames and back again. In 1963 a new terminal was built further from the centre of Woolwich and new piers were added in 1966.

The author and playwright, Enid Bagnold (1889-1981) (great-grandmother of Samantha Cameron, wife of the present Prime Minister), who lived at Shooter's Hill when her father was stationed at Woolwich, remembered the ferries: 'One loaded while the other crossed. The one that arrived let down its ramp and the horses, carts and lorries went on first, bumping up the wooden planks. It was ten minutes each way and ten minutes to wait. One bank you knew: the other was 'foreign'. Then the reverse. And once out on the river, silver, black or scarlet, depending on the hour, both banks had a fringe, at angles, of cranes looking like trees.' It is not so different today.

The Woolwich Foot Tunnel is an alternative way to cross the river. It was built at the instigation of Will Crooks (1852-1921), who spent part of his early life in the workhouse, worked in the docks, and later entered politics, becoming the first ever Labour mayor in London (Mayor of Poplar), Labour MP for Woolwich and a Privy Councillor.

Crooks was concerned that when the free ferries could not run due to foggy weather, workers who needed to cross the Thames could lose a whole day's work and were sometimes dismissed by their employers as a result. With the new tunnel they could always get to the other side.

ABOVE The old Station Museum, North Woolwich.

BELOW The entrance to the Woolwich Foot Tunnel.

The tunnel leads from North Woolwich in the borough of Newham to Woolwich in the borough of Greenwich. It was opened in 1912. It is 504 meters long and accessed by stairs and lifts from circular buildings on either side of the river, with glass domes. The north entrance stands prominently in the open air, but the south entrance is somewhat overshadowed by the modern building work of the Waterfront leisure centre.

From now on the Thames is a feature of the Greenway route, which follows it in all the next sections from 8 to 11. To the left (east) the River heads towards the sea, while to the right (west) towards the Thames Flood Barrier and Central London.

Section 8 – Woolwich to Greenwich

This Section follows the Thames Path and stays close to the river except where building works prevent this. It has some stunning landmarks and breathtaking views.

It starts at Woolwich, originally in Kent but since 1889 part of the Royal Borough of Greenwich. Woolwich played a leading role in Britain's military past. The Royal Arsenal dates from 1471, the Woolwich Dockyard was founded by Henry VIII in 1512, the Royal Military Academy in 1741 and the Royal Horse Artillery in 1793. There is still an army base at Royal Artillery Barracks (where the shooting events of 2012 Games take place) and the Royal Artillery Museum celebrates the history of that regiment. The Greenwich Heritage Centre has exhibits connected to the Royal Arsenal.

The famous Building Society – the Woolwich – was the original home of Arsenal Football Club, founded in 1886 by workers at the Arsenal (but which later moved to Highbury). The Woolwich Polytechnic was founded in 1892 and became Thames Polytechnic in 1970. In 1992 it became the University of Greenwich and relocated in the

The O2 Dome on the south bank of the Thames.

Old Royal Naval College at Greenwich. The first ever branch of McDonald's in Britain opened in Woolwich.

Amongst famous residents the diarist, Samuel Pepys, took lodgings in Woolwich in 1665 to avoid the Great Plague of London.

On arrival at Woolwich, whether by ferry or via the tunnel, the pedestrian or cyclist will follow the Thames Path east towards Central London. The route is undeniably something of a muddle at many points due to extensive construction work. Here there is room for improvement and this will come about, inspired in part by being along the Jubilee Greenway, just as the Jubilee Walkway helped to create The Queen's Walk between 1977 and 1994.

The Thames is such a feature of the walk and this part leads from Woolwich Reach to Blackwall Reach and round to Greenwich Reach.

In 8000 BC England was still joined to Europe by land. In 889 AD the first wharf property was recorded at Greenhithe. In 1269 there was a Great Frost, and in 1564 another, enabling people to walk on the ice between London Bridge and Westminster. In 1577 Francis Drake sailed down the Thames from Deptford on his voyage to circumnavigate the world.

In the 1800s, a time of industrial growth, factories were built alongside the river and by the 1920s some

200 ferries were plying their way along its navigable length. Until 1957 there were no fish in the Thames due to pollution and sewerage, but now there are over 100 species and it is the cleanest metropolitan river in Europe. Yet the river flows somewhat brown because mud moves with the flow. The Thames salmon rehabilitation scheme reintroduced salmon in 1982 and now there are adult eels as far as Tower Bridge, jellied eels are traditionally a staple diet of the East End. Thin-lipped grey mullet can be spotted in the spring as far up river as Woolwich. A whitebait factory flourished at Greenwich until the early 1800s – and the Trafalgar Tavern, next to the Royal Naval College, still boasts whitebait dinners.

Across the river can be seen many satellite dishes and in the distance ahead the Thames Barrier, the Dome, and the great financial buildings of Canary Wharf. Nearby are the large modern flats of Mast Quay. A housing estate now stands on the site of the Royal Dockyard, Woolwich, built by Henry VIII in 1512.

The Thames Path National Trail runs 290km along the Thames from its source to the Thames Barrier. In 2001 it was unofficially extended to Crayfordness.

Heading east, there is a rondel in the ground, with mosaics – marked Riverside Walk Project 1984–1986 and National Elfrida Rathbone Society. Around it are listed the months of the year. On some steps to the left, there are some sculpted fishes in the stonework and, ahead, two cannons. The route passes many disused basins, crosses cycle bridges and footbridges and housing estates of varying distinction. In due course it crosses the busy Woolwich Road (the A206) and then Maryon Park on the left. This park houses Cox's Mount, a Roman hillfort (discovered as recently as 1915). In 1966 some dramatic scenes in Antonioni's film, *Blowup* (1966) were filmed here. Today it sports hard tennis courts, a basketball court, and a children's play area.

Presently it is possible to rejoin the Thames Path – pedestrians before the Thames Flood Barrier and cyclists after it. Work on the Thames Flood Barrier began in 1974 and it was officially opened on 9 May 1984, though first used defensively in 1983. Its purpose is to prevent flooding in Central London

ABOVE Nelson's Tavern at Greenwich.

BELOW One of the basins near Woolwich, with modern flats behind.

due to unusually high tides caused by storm surges at sea and it has been thus used 100 times. On 9 November 2007 it was closed twice.

The Barrier stretches right across the Thames, some 572 metres, dividing the river into four 200 metre sections and two 34-metre navigable spans. There are also four smaller non-navigable channels, with altogether 9 concrete piers and 2 abutments. The floodgates are raised by hydraulics from a horizontal sill on the riverbed and form a barrier of steel and concrete. Being hollow, and made of steel, the gates fill with water when submerged and empty as they emerge from the river.

From now on the route stays close to the Thames, heading to the O2 Dome and curving round it, with occasional diversions, on its way to Greenwich.

ABOVE The Thames Barrier.

BELOW Anthony Gormley's sculpture Quantum Cloud near the Dome.

It passes the Greenwich Yacht Club (founded by Greenwich watermen and people who worked on the river in 1908) and the Ecology Park, a long-term regeneration project which brought 121 hectares of derelict land back to life. It reaches Greenwich Peninsular, formerly the site of enormous gasworks but now transformed as a Millennium initiative and re-landscaped to provide 2,900 new homes, a school, a health centre and supermarket and the new North Greenwich Underground and Bus Station, designed by Lord Rodgers.

There is the David Beckham or London Academy, opened in 2005 with two full-sized football pitches, part of the national schools programme during term time and offering a variety of training programmes for boys and girls between 8 and 15 during school holidays.

Millennium Square connects the Underground and Bus Station to the entrance of the Dome and affords possibilities for live performances and other outdoor events. Beside the river is Queen Elizabeth II Pier, serving the O2 Dome, where the Thames Clipper lands every 20 minutes, bringing passengers from Central London. On a nearby platform, rising from the river, stands Anthony Gormley's sculpture, Quantum Cloud, made from 3,500 steel tubes, and described as embodying 'a radical vision of the

human being as a zone of light and energy'.

The O2 Dome is one of the great landmarks along the Jubilee Greenway with its white roof and yellow spikes pointing skyward. Designed by Lord Foster to celebrate the Millennium, it comprises a 23,000-seat arena for music and sport, which was the venue for basketball and gymnastic events in the London 2012 Games. The Dome also includes many restaurants, bars, exhibition areas, cinemas, interactive experiences, and other leisure facilities.

The Dome had controversial beginnings. Originally commissioned by the Conservative Government as a celebration of the Millennium, it became a project for New Labour when they were elected to government in 1997. Labour Prime Minister, Tony Blair, declared in 1998: 'This will be the most famous new building in the world.' He invited The Queen and The Duke of Edinburgh to the Dome to see in the new Millennium on New Year's Eve 1999/2000. The Dome appears in the James Bond film, *The World is Not Enough* (1999), when Bond ends up there after a memorable river chase.

The route circles the Dome at Blackwall Point, under which the 1897 Blackwall Tunnel (in fact two tunnels, one for vehicles and another for pedestrians) passes under the Thames, connecting East Greenwich

The O2 Dome.

to Blackwall. This stretch of the river is Blackwall Reach. From here the great financial buildings on Canary Wharf are in full view. Canary Wharf stands on the Isle of Dogs, thought to be so named because Edward III housed his greyhounds there. Others have suggested that it was just a pejorative term for the empty marshlands. Now a major financial centre, it used to house the largest of the docks.

Along this stretch are nesting piers and jetties to

ABOVE The disused Alcatel Jetty, East Greenwich, is planted with flowers and is a haven for wildlife.

RIGHT The Cutty Sark pub.

provide a safe habitat for wildlife. A great number of wharves are passed which used to house gunpowder magazines, submarine cables, Portland stone and Purbeck marble, and were used for the building of ships and yachts, loading gravel and coal.

Presently the Royal Naval College at Greenwich looms in the distance. Moving onwards, a wide L-shaped jetty affords great views over the river, to Greenwich on the left, and the Dome on the right. This is the East Greenwich riverfront.

The land here was given by King Edgar to the Abbey of St Peter's in Ghent, Flanders, in 964. Henry V repossessed it in 1414, and after the Civil War, in 1676, Charles II granted the land to Sir William Boreman, Clerk to the Board of Green Cloth, a man instrumental in the design of Greenwich Park.

This varied part of the route has its share of graffiti-covered buildings – a disused jetty, the Alcatel Jetty, planted with mosses and sedums (stonecrops) as a habitat for birds, including heron, black redstarts and cormorants.

Later there are Georgian houses at Union Wharf and the Cutty Sark pub, built in about 1795 on Ballast Quay. The riverside walk has been resurfaced and widened here, and Berkeley Homes were opened in 2003. A stray anchor survives from Anchor Iron Wharf.

As the path moves on, Greenwich Power Station looms overhead on the left. This is a large building with great chimneys built for the London County Council in 1906 to provide power for LCC trams, still operational today, acting as back-up for power in the Underground. Just beyond is Trinity Hospital, an almshouse built in 1616 by Henry Howard, Earl of Northampton, now housing 21 local people.

Before Greenwich there is the Curlew Rowing Club (1866) then *The Yacht* (advertised as the first pub in the West Longitude), followed by the Trafalgar Tavern Club (famed for its whitebait dinners, with a Nelson Room and Admiral's Gallery). Literary figures such as William Thackeray, Wilkie Collins and Charles Dickens frequented it, and Dickens set the wedding day breakfast scene there in *Our Mutual Friend*.

Outside the Trafalgar Tavern is a statue of Admiral Lord Nelson who died at the Battle of Trafalgar in 1805. His body was conveyed up the Thames and he lay in state at the Great Hall in Greenwich. 20,000 people came to pay their respects, and a further 60,000 had to be turned away. Later his body was again taken by river to St Paul's Cathedral for his funeral and burial.

At this point there are fine views back to the Dome and across to Island Gardens on the Isle of Dogs and to the left, Greenwich itself, the Royal Naval College dominating the view, with the Royal Steps in front, leading down to the Thames.

Greenwich was declared a Maritime World Heritage site by UNESCO. It stands at the Prime Meridian on Longitude 0 0, and is the site of Greenwich Meantime. In celebration of the Diamond Jubilee, it has been declared to be a Royal Borough, the first new one since 1928.

Sir Walter Scott wrote: 'There are two things scarce matched in the universe, the sun in heaven, and the Thames on earth. The one will light us to Greenwich, and the other would take us there a little faster, if it were ebb-tide.' Edward Walford described Greenwich as 'the finest specimen of classical architecture in this or almost any other country.'

Dominating the waterfront is the Royal Naval College, built on a horseshoe-bend on the Thames, with extensive views both up and down stream. It holds a commanding position, which had strategic advantages in time of war, and was impressive when greeting foreign royal visitors in time of peace. Twice every 24 hours, the ocean waters surge from

Trinity Hospital, an almshouse built in 1616.

the North Sea and lap the palace walls. In olden times, the river was a safer means of transport than the roads, and as such the Thames was the main thoroughfare through London.

Greenwich's history has been closely associated with the Kings and Queens of England since its earliest times. King Harold held manors there, and it was a royal residence as early as the reign of Edward I. The first chapter of the Order of the Garter was held in the Great Hall at Greenwich by Edward III, and he travelled to Woolwich by barge to name the ship, *Elizabeth Jonas*. Great Duke Humphrey, the Duke of Gloucester and Regent for Henry VI, embattled the manor of Greenwich and erected a tower within on the site of the present Observatory. Richard, Duke of York, father of Edward IV, married Anne Mowbray there, and Henry VII completed the tower in the park.

Henry VIII was born here in 1491 and held jousts and water pageants. He married Katharine of Aragon here and his daughters, Queen Mary I and later Elizabeth I (daughter of Anne Boleyn) were born at Greenwich. It was here that Sir Walter Raleigh threw his plush red cloak to the ground for Elizabeth I to step on, during a visit following his triumphal return from Ireland. (Later, it was at Greenwich that he was intercepted after his Guiana trip and conducted to the Tower of London).

The Royal Naval College, Greenwich.

From Greenwich Anne Boleyn set off heading as she thought to Whitehall, only to be diverted into the Traitors' Gate at the Tower of London and subsequently executed there. Henry VIII brought Jane Seymour to Greenwich and received Francis I, King of France here. Edward VI, his son by Jane Seymour, was born at Greenwich and died here in 1553.

James I settled Greenwich on his wife, Anne of Denmark. Queen Henrietta Maria completed 'The House of Delight' – now known as the Queen's House (more Georgian than Jacobean), designed by Inigo Jones and built between 1629 and 1635. Charles I held court at Greenwich and then in 1652 it was sold under the Commonwealth. In 1660, after the Restoration, Charles II had the old Greenwich pulled down and designed a new palace. He completed one wing and also laid out the park with formal avenues between 1661 and 1662, with

Le Nôtre as his gardener. The Queen's House was enlarged by John Webb in 1662.

In 1692 Queen Mary II declared that Greenwich should become a 'retreat for seamen disabled in the service of their country,' and thus it became the Royal Naval Hospital, serving as such until 1869, after which it became Greenwich Naval College. Since 1873 the Hospital had been run by the Royal Naval College, which had taken over the original hospital for old sailors. After the University of Greenwich took it over, there has been free admission to the Painted Hall, attracting 300,000 visitors a year.

In the present reign, there was a memorable day in the summer of 1967, when The Queen came to Greenwich to knight Sir Francis Chichester, following his successful lone voyage round the world.

Wren designed the monument to William III. The statue of George II is by John Michael Rysbrach and was erected in 1735. There is a statue of William IV by Samuel Nixon, which originally towered over London Bridge, on the junction of King William

Street and Gracechurch Street but was removed in 1935 and the following year mounted on a new pedestal, at King William's Walk in Greenwich Park.

In 1995 there was fear that Greenwich Hospital might be sold. A campaign was raised by the late Admiral of the Fleet Lord Lewin (1920-99) against the Major Government. There were fears that students at the University of Greenwich might cover the fine buildings by Wren, Vanbrugh and Hawksmoor in graffiti.

The opposite happened. The Greenwich Foundation has done magnificent restoration work. They installed Trinity College of Music in the King Charles Block, providing music for Greenwich chapel. A 55 metre observation wheel is open during the summer season, from the top of which there are views as far as Highgate and Hampstead and it is possible to observe the Lea Valley and Blackheath over the crest of Greenwich Hill.

Section 9 – Greenwich to Tower Bridge

This Section stretches from the great Palace of Greenwich along the South Bank of the Thames, following the Thames Path, curving round and eventually passing through Bermondsey to Tower Bridge. Some of it is unexciting, and with development and rebuilding always on the go, the route frequently veers away from the river.

The route starts with the grandeur of Greenwich and ends as Central London approaches. In between, the way is best described as various. Some of it is still quite run down but as it approaches Rotherhithe so the residential buildings become smarter and more expensive and finally it passes stylish restaurants and Tower Bridge is reached.

At Greenwich there are various points of interest. There are the Lewin Gates (named after the Admiral of the Fleet and opened in 2003 by The Duke of Edinburgh who served with him in the Royal Navy). Greenwich Foot Tunnel is a pedestrian foot tunnel

The Greenway making its way along the Thames Path between the Dome and Greenwich.

which leads under the Thames to the Isle of Dogs and emerges next to Island Gardens. It was commissioned by the London County Council, designed by Sir Alexander Binnie and opened in 1902.

Cutty Sark was built at Dumbarton in Scotland in 1869 as a tea clipper, the last clipper ever built as a merchant vessel. She achieved the record of the fastest passage from London to Sydney in 1874. In 1895 she was sold to the Portuguese firm, Ferreira, then dismasted in 1916 and sold in Cape Town. In 1922 Captain William Dowman bought her and restored her to her original appearance. The Duke of Edinburgh set up the Cutty Sark Society (later Trust) in 1951 and saved her. In 1954 she was moved to the present custom-built dry dock at Greenwich.

In 1957 The Queen opened her as a museum, but she was badly damaged by fire in 2007, while partly dismantled for construction work. Fortunately at least half her timbers were not on site. An additional £5-10 million was needed for her restoration, bringing the total to around £35 million. In January 2008 the Heritage Lottery Fund awarded the Cutty Sark Trust an extra £10 million, and an Israeli shipping magnate, Sammy Ofer, made up the balance needed. *Cutty Sark* was restored in time for reopening by The Queen in April 2012.

The route passes over Deptford Creek suspension bridge, over the mouth of the River Ravensbourne,

first bridged in 1804. It passes a statue of Russian Czar, Peter the Great, recording his only visit to England in 1698 to study shipbuilding and staying mainly in Deptford.

Deptford was the home of Deptford Dockyard and Royal Victoria Yard. Royal ships were repaired here as early as 1420. Henry VIII built the Great Storehouse here for the Navy. In King's Yard some 350 Royal Naval vessels were built between 1545 and 1869. Then the Dockyard was closed, and later it was variously a foreign cattle market and a Navy victualling and supply centre before being redeveloped in the 1970s.

There are various docks, such as South Dock and neighbouring Greenland Dock. South Dock, built between 1807 and 1811, is the last of the former Surrey Commercial Docks to survive. It was gravely damaged by Luftwaffe bombing in the Second World War. The Surrey Docks closed in 1970. Most were filled in but South Dock survived to become London's largest marina with more than 200 berths for yachts and residential barges.

Greenland Dock was formerly the Howland Great Wet Dock, an early fitting-out basin laid out between 1695 and 1699 on land belonging to 1st Duke of Bedford. It is the oldest of London's riverside docks and was used for the refitting of East India ships. Later it was used by the Greenland whaling ships. In 1806 it was sold to William Richie, a Greenwich timber merchant. Only one entrance now remains, but the old capstans and hydraulic machines remain on the quayside.

Nelson Dock was a dry dock used for shipbuilding from the 17th century until 1968. War ships and clippers were built here.

Rotherhithe is opposite Wapping and the Isle of Dogs. It was originally a series of islands, surrounded by marsh. The name is thought to come from the Saxon 'Rother' meaning cattle and 'Hythe' meaning a landing place. It has been a port since the 12th century and a shipyard since Elizabethan times. Rotherhithe was the birth place of Max Bygraves and of Sir Michael Caine. In the late 1950s the photographer Antony Armstrong-Jones had a riverside house here, which his future wife, Princess Margaret, used to visit.

By the 1980s most of the docks had closed and many had been filled in and the area developed for housing and other commercial ventures.

There are two tunnels – the Thames Tunnel to Wapping, originally a Mark Brunel built foot tunnel (opened in 1843), later taken over by the Underground (the East London Line). The Rotherhithe Tunnel was opened in 1908 and is a

two-lane road to Limehouse. There is also a Jubilee Line extension (opened in 1999) to Canary Wharf and the Isle of Dogs.

Various other wharves are passed, amongst which Globe Wharf, built in 1883, is one of the finest listed warehouses surviving in the docks. Next door is King & Queen Wharf, formerly Bellamy's Wharf, built by French prisoners during the Napoleonic Wars in the 1790's. The Mayflower Pub at Rotherhithe was restored in 1957 and given its present name. Before that it was the Spread Eagle & Crown and originally the Shippe. It was from here that *Mayflower* set sail in the spring of 1620 with a group of Protestants on board, fleeing religious persecution. The captain was Christopher Jones, and with him at the helm, they reached Plymouth, Massachusetts and became the Pilgrim Fathers. *Mayflower* and its crew returned to Rotherhithe in 1621. Jones died here a year later and was buried in St Mary's Churchyard, just opposite the pub.

The route passes St Mary's Church, Rotherhithe, a Church of England church in the diocese of Southwark, rebuilt by John James, an associate of Sir Christopher Wren. Southwark Park (a 63-acre park opened in 1863) is to the left of King's Stairs Gardens beside the river. Here can be seen a plinth celebrating the Silver and Golden Jubilee, unveiled by The Earl and Countess of Wessex on 5 July 2002.

Next comes St Saviour's Dock, a small dock to the east of Tower Bridge, next to Shad Thames, at the point where the River Neckinger enters the Thames. It was made into a dock by the Cluniac monks at Bermondsey Abbey. Beyond it is Jacob's Island, the site of some of Bermondsey's worst mid-19th century slums, many of which were the settings for scenes in the novels of Charles Dickens. Bill Sikes, the murderer in *Oliver Twist*, had his den here and fell to his death in the mud, possibly even into St Saviour's Dock. It is all much smarter now.

Continuing eastwards is the Design Museum, one of the world's leading museums of modern and contemporary design. Since its foundation in 1989 it has won international acclaim for exhibitions on modern design history and contemporary design.

The route follows Shad Thames, a picturesque and historic street running along the river near Tower Bridge. Here are many famous and smart restaurants, including Le Pont de la Tour, where Prime Minister Tony Blair and his wife entertained President and Mrs Clinton of the USA in 1997.

This section ends at Tower Bridge.

Section 10 – Tower Bridge to South Bank Lion
This Section continues along the Thames Path and joins the original route of the Jubilee Walkway. For this section, please see The Jubilee Walkway Route.

Section 11 – South Bank Lion to Buckingham Palace
This Section leads further along the South Bank to Lambeth Bridge, then to Parliament Square, St James's Park and up Birdcage Walk past the Guards Chapel to Buckingham Palace.

Section 12 – The Mile End Route Victoria Park to Limehouse Basin

This is an extra Section of the Jubilee Greenway. It leads from the easterly corner of Victoria Park (where Section 5 meets Section 6) down to Limehouse Basin. It is a particularly attractive route, easy to follow and shows the close proximity of stark urban development to a relatively rustic environment.

This way starts at Victoria Park but does not enter the park itself. It continues along the towpath of the

The old towpath along the Mile End Loop of the Grand Union Canal.

Regent's Canal, under Bonner Bridge (the formal entrance to Victoria Park) and Ford Road, where the canal becomes the Grand Union Canal and heads south. It continues along the towpath, passes under Roman Road, through Mile End and under several other bridges until it reaches the harbour complex of Limehouse Basin. Here the canal joins the River Thames. At one time this was the main thoroughfare for transporting goods by narrow boat through London and linking with the other canals.

It passes Mile End Park to the left. Formerly 'a ragged series of small parks strung out along the Grand Union Canal and broken up by roads and railways,' the park has been united by a central pathway linking separate themed sections – art, sport, play, ecology and fun. A 'green bridge' was built over the A11, enabling people to cross that major highway without realising it. New buildings were carefully integrated into the landscape. This park, funded by the Millennium Commission and others, links Victoria Park in the north to the Limehouse Cut, and passes through the Docks to Island Gardens in the south. It also contains King George's Field and the Mile End Stadium.

This extra section ends at Limehouse Basin, a navigable link between the Regent's Canal and the Thames, which used to cover an area of 15 acres. It was previously called Regent's Canal Dock and was where the cargo arrived on ships up the River Thames to be transferred onto canal barges for the voyage up the Grand Union Canal and Regent's Canal. When it first opened in 1820, it was a failure, but gradually trade picked up and by the mid 19th century it was transporting coal and other commodities. At one point it was the principal entrance to the Thames for the national canal network.

Today it is a harbour for expensive yachts, surrounded by huge blocks of luxury apartments. This redevelopment began in 1983 as part of the London Docklands Development Corporation's master plan for the Docklands Area. By early 2004 most of the derelict land to the north had been developed. It is a striking example of how greatly London has changed in recent years.

* * * * *

The Regent's Canal heading to Limehouse.

The Jubilee Greenway is a most varied route. It is possible to move quickly between different areas from the quiet and grandly residential to trading markets and in some cases into areas which are considerably rundown. To walk all of it is to pass through many varied socio-economic areas. By so doing, it is clear that London is never static for

Limehouse Basin, once the gateway for commerce to the canals, now a marina.

RIGHT Despite the looming presence of Canary Wharf and the rattle of the trains on the Docklands Light Railway, the Regent's Canal is still a peaceful urban haven.

long. The old cranes on the South Bank of recent memory have given way to smart reconstructions. The damage inflicted on London by the Luftwaffe in the Second World War has been repaired. The glass towers of the financial sector dwarf Wren's churches and St Paul's Cathedral and the Tower of London is no longer a dominant feature in the City. We live in the age of the Gherkin and the Shard. But there is something for everybody who is prepared to set off and walk this 60-kilometre route.

On 29 February 2012 a few minutes were granted outside Buckingham Palace in which to encapsulate what the Jubilee Walkway and Greenway are. This is an edited version of what I said:

It is curious to realise that the origins of the new Jubilee Greenway and of the original Jubilee Walkway date back to the Festival of Britain in 1951 in which Max Nicholson and other Trustees played such a key part. Max dreamt up the idea of the Jubilee Walkway to get people walking on the South Bank. King George VI took a liking to the stone lion outside the Red Lion Brewery (which was pulled down for the Festival Hall) so much so that the lion now stands proudly on the South Bank by Westminster Bridge. The Queen opened the Jubilee Walkway there on 9 June 1977, uniting the cities of Westminster and London.

As related, it took a further 17 years to run the Walkway along the South Bank of the Thames thus creating The Queen's Walk again opened by the Queen in October 1994.

For the Golden Jubilee all the Panoramic, panels were revised and the Jubilee Walkway extended up the Mall.

The new route, the Jubilee Greenway, starts at Buckingham Palace. It goes up Constitution Hill through Hyde Park to Kensington, up the Broad Walk – along Bayswater to Paddington to the Pool of Little Venice. It then follows the Regent's Canal all the way to Victoria Park, created between 1842 and 1846 in response to a petition from 30,000 residents of the East End who asked Queen

Victoria for a Royal Park in the Queen's name as 'a Monument to future generations'.

The lock between the Regent's Canal and Limehouse.

The route continues through the main Olympic site at Stratford, along and down to Beckton and the river, crosses at Woolwich, and then follows the Thames Path to join the Jubilee Walkway at Tower Bridge – and back to the Palace.

The route is 60 kilometres long – appropriately. It is marked with 500 discs, the first and last of which are between the central gates of Buckingham Palace. Queen Victoria only saw her park once in 1873 but we hope that The Queen will see this disc often as she comes and goes to the Palace through the central gates for the State Opening of Parliament, Trooping the Colour and State Visits.

The Jubilee Greenway is a gift to The Queen in celebration of the Diamond Jubilee, and in a wider sense it is a gift to all those in London who will enjoy walking it in the years to come.

The work of the Trust is done but we do not intend to be idle. Under the auspices of Walk England, we will take advantage of numerous ways in which to promote the routes. We hope to create further routes in other towns and in Commonwealth countries, using our accumulated experience to encourage people to walk, to enjoy and understand the environs through which they pass and to appreciate the architectural features and the views. For walking is a means to good health, keeps the body in good shape and by following these routes we can further enrich the mind and our appreciation of London's history.

We can build on the 35 years of work undertaken by the Trust. There are exciting challenges ahead.

* * * * *

Appendices

I THE ENVIRONMENTAL COMMITTEE

In 2009 the Environmental (Greening) Committee was formalised under the chairmanship of Joyce Bellamy. She co-opted William Crossley, Chris Patey and Dr John Parker to assist her. This was a way to develop work which had been ongoing for many years in order to further adorn the Walkway by planting trees, donating benches, and giving plants to various institutions along the Walkway.

Joyce Bellamy had long been keen to remind appropriate institutions of their proximity to the Walkway and her efforts produced sponsorship, funding and mutual promotion. This was particularly important during occasional quiet periods in the Trust's history when there were no panel unveilings or major events to celebrate. On many occasions the Trust's meetings were hosted in places such as the Museum of Garden History, Tate Modern, the Jerusalem Chamber of Westminster Abbey, the Maughan Library at King's College, London and other imaginative venues.

Achievements in this category included the planting of a cherry tree (sponsored by London Transport) by The Duke of Gloucester in St James's Park in March 2000. This marked the start of renovation work to the Walkway and the completion of the London Underground's Jubilee extension. The event echoed The Queen's original planting of an oak tree in 1977 and inspired further such plantings along the route of the Jubilee Walkway in the years that followed. At his own request, the Duke later took a tour of the Jubilee Underground to see the imaginative designs of the new stations.

Then the Chairman planted the Temple Bar tree in 2005; assistance was given to a 'green wall' for the new conservation building of the British Library and a bench given to Woburn Square in 2007, which

ABOVE The Duke of Gloucester planting a tree in St James's Park in March 2000.

BELOW The Canons of Southwark Cathedral enjoying their bench in the Cathedral's Millennium Garden in September 2010.

prompted a visit to Gordon and Woburn Squares by The Princess Royal, Chancellor of the University of London, to mark the refurbishment of those squares, which enhanced public access.

Bulbs were planted in St Mary's Garden near Lambeth Bridge, when it was refurbished and the bulbs flowered for the first time in the spring of 2009.

A bench was placed in the garden of Westminster Abbey and unveiled by Very Rev Dr John Hall, Dean of Westminster, in December 2009, a way of thanking him for hosting the meeting in the crypt of the Abbey in November 2007. Climbing plants were given to the community garden at Tate Modern as a thank you gift for allowing the Trust to hold an AGM in one of their committee rooms. A bench was placed in the Millennium Garden of Southwark Cathedral in September 2010, following the Cathedral's Patronal Service, attended by a good compliment of Trustees and including an act of dedication held in the open air near the bench.

A further tree was planted by the Chairman in Chancery Lane in September 2011 to mark the completion of the recent refurbishment project by the Cities of London and Westminster and the Borough of Camden to revitalise Chancery Lane. This included the creation of a sitting area as a resting point for users of the Walkway and others.

As with so many activities of the Trust, each planting or bench was the result of site-by-site discussion and on many occasions the recipients were delighted to find that by being near the Walkway they could become involved and even receive the unexpected benefit of a tree, bulbs or a bench.

2 THE TRUSTEES

The Walkway has been fortunate in the Trustees who guided it over several decades. In 2012 only one of the original Trustees, Kate Trevelyan, was still serving, though arguably Sir James Swaffield had been actively involved from the start. Two served since 1986 and three from the 1990s. Since 2006 no new Trustees were appointed, since it seemed inappropriate to do so if the Trust was to be wound up.

The Trustees brought a breadth of experience to the deliberations of the Trust, coming variously from government, the GLC, the Civic Trust, the City of London, the world of architects and various other areas of life, each adding something special. Many of the early Trustees were involved with the London Celebrations Committee and several dated right back to the Festival of Britain in 1951.

PATRON
HRH The Duke of Gloucester, KG, GCVO – from 1978

CHAIRMEN
Robert Shaw, LVO – 1978-95
Neville Labovitch, LVO, MBE – 1995-2001 (President 2001-2)
Sir James Swaffield, CBE, RD – 2001-2
Hugo Vickers, DL – from 2002

TRUSTEES
Robert Shaw LVO (1913-95) – Trustee 1978-95, Chairman 1978-95. Former Assistant Chief Planner, GLC, Member of Environmental Committee, London Celebrations Committee.

Neville Labovitch, LVO, MBE (1927-2002) – Trustee 1978-2001, Vice-Chairman 1978-95, Chairman 1995-2001, President 2001-2. Chairman Piccadilly Tourist Trust, Knightsbridge Association & Cleaner London Campaign; Member of Environmental Committee, London Celebrations Committee.

George Chandler, CBE (1914-91) – Trustee 1978-91. Former City Architect, Corporation of London; City Architect, Oxford; Common Counsellor; Master of the Worshipful Company of Gardiners.

Peter Drew, OBE (1927-2007) – Trustee 1978-2007. Chairman and Managing Director St Katharine-by-the-Tower; Director International World Trade Centre Movement.

Robert Green, MBE (b. 1917) – Trustee 1978-95 – hon Treasurer 1978-95 (resigned). Retired Accountant; former Assistant Treasurer, GLC.

David Hamilton (1930-85) – Trustee 1978 – (officially) 1986; hon Secretary 1983 – (officially) 1986, Ceremonial Officer, GLC; Head of Chairman's Office. He was murdered in 1985.

George Mann, OBE (1915-2004) – Trustee 1978-83 (resigned). Former Director, South Bank Concert Halls, GLC.

Michael Middleton, CBE (1917-2009) – Trustee 1978-2007, Vice-Chairman 1995-8, Trustee Emeritus 2007-9. Director, The Civic Trust 1969-86 (Secretary and Deputy Director 1957-69); formerly art critic of *The Spectator*; art editor and assistant editor, *Picture Post*; executive editor, *Lilliput*; & Editor of *House and Garden* 1955-7; Member of the Council of Industrial Society; & of Society of Industrial Artists and Designers; UK Secretary-General European Architectural Heritage Year 1972-5; Member of Environmental Committee, London Celebrations Committee.

Lord Ponsonby of Shulbrede (1930-90) – Trustee 1978-90. Chairman, London Convention Board 1977-83; & formerly of London Tourist Board 1976-80; Leader of the Labour Group, GLC 1976-7; Labour Councillor, Kensington & Chelsea 1956-65, & Alderman 1964-74; Opposition Whip, House of Lords 1979-81 & Deputy Chief Opposition Whip 1981-2; spearheaded *Clean Up London* campaign. In *Who's Who* he listed his recreations as 'eating, drinking, window-box gardening'.

The Duke of Gloucester with the Jubilee Walkway team on board *Golden Jubilee*, 29 February 2012. Left to right: William Crossley, Chris Patey, Kate Trevelyan, Jenny Humphreys, Hugo Vickers, The Duke of Gloucester, Andrew Dent, Nicky Gavron, Sir James Swaffield, Dr John Parker, Joyce Bellamy and Jim Walker.

Anthony Prendergast, CBE, DL (1931-98) – Trustee 1978-98. Town planner; Lord Mayor of Westminster and Deputy High Sheriff of London, 1968-9; High Sheriff of Greater London, 1980; Chairman Town Planning Committee, City of Westminster, 1972-5; member of Westminster City Council 1959-90; member of London Boroughs Training Committee, 1965-8; & of the Docklands Development Committee 1974; Chairman, Location of Office Bureaus, 1971-9; Chairman of the Dolphin Square Trust. Married to Dame Simone Prendergast, DBE, DL, JP, Lady Mayoress of Westminster 1968-9.

Sir Paul (later Lord) Reilly (1912-90) – Trustee 1978-90. Director, Design Council, 1960-77; created Life Peer, 1978; member Environmental Committee, London Celebrations Committee.

Company 1990-1. He was killed crossing the road at Woodford Green High Road, returning to his home from a City of London function.

Maureen, Lady Ponsonby of Shulbrede (b. 1932) – Trustee 1991-2001 (resigned). Maureen Campbell-Teich, married to Lord Ponsonby, as his 3rd wife 1973. Barrister & Arbitrator. Widowed 1990. Went to live abroad.

Christopher Patey, MBE (b. 1937) – Trustee from 1995-7, & from 1998, Director 1997-8. Former Oil Company Executive; Trustee, Chelsea Opera Group; Treasurer, Friends of Southwark Cathedral; Chairman, the Oil Depletion Analysis Centre; Chairman, Wimbledon Decorative and Fine Arts Society; member of Joyce Bellamy's Greening Committee.

Geoffrey Price (b. 1934) – Trustee 1995-2009 (resigned), Hon Treasurer 1995-2005. Local Government Chief Executive; previously a Borough treasurer.

Raymond Andrews, MBE (1925-99) – Trustee 1996-9. Senior Partner of Andrews, Downie & Partners, and a former Vice-President of the Royal Institute of British Architects from 1972 to 1974. It was hoped that his knowledge of urban design would help the Trust, to some extent compensating for the loss of Robert Shaw. All too soon, Mr Andrews died in October 1999, aged 74.

George Banks (b. 1933) – Trustee from 1999. Director General of Corgi 1974-98; commenced work in the gas industry 1951; formed part of the Guard of Honour at St Paul's Cathdedral for the Proclamation of The Queen, 1952; Past Master, Worshipful Company of Plumbers; Chairman of Government Working Party on statutory registration scheme for gas installers since privatisation of British Gas 1986; Past President of the Institute of Plumbing; Companion of the Institution of Gas Engineers.

Councillor Peter Truesdale (b. 1937) – Trustee 1999-2001 (resigned). Liberal Councillor for Lambeth since 1994; Leader of the Liberal Democrats on Lambeth Council; with Esso UK plc 1980-91; joined their Corporate Affairs Department, member of Community Action Programme, left Esso 1998; member of Jubilee Gardens Committee.

Ian Liddell (1933-2001) – Trustee 2000-1 Architect with Design Research Unit.

Hugo Vickers, DL (b. 1951), – Trustee from 2000, Vice-Chairman 2001-2, Chairman from 2002. Author, broadcaster, lecturer & royal historian; Lay Steward, St George's Chapel, Windsor from 1970; steward at Windsor Festival 1969-80 (Festival Marshal 1974-80); worked with the London Celebrations Committee 1977, Administrator of the Great Children's Party, Hyde Park, 1979; Member of Prince of Wales's Tree Committee 1987-2003.

Nicolette (Nicky) Gavron (b. 1939) – Trustee from 2002. Deputy Mayor of London 2000-3; Labour Member, London Assembly, GLA, from 2000; member Haringey Borough Council 1986-2002, Member & Leader Labour Group, London Planning Advisory Committee 1989-97; & 1998-2000; Chairman, National Planning Forum 1999-2002.

Dr John Parker (b. 1933) – Trustee from 2002. Chartered Architect, town Planner and urban designer; formerly Project Architect at LCC 1961-64; Group Leader Urban Design, London Borough of Lambeth 1964-70; Planning Architect for Central London 1970-83 and Head of the Central Area Team 1983-86 GLC. Founded Greater London Consultants, 1986; John Parker Associates, 1996; member of Joyce Bellamy's Greening Committee.

Andrew Dent, MVO (b. 1964) – Trustee from 2004. Spent three years in the Private Office at Buckingham Palace and then led delivery at the Golden Jubilee Office in the summer of 2002; Deputy Director National Asylum Support Service until 2005; Director Identity Cards Programme, Home Office until 2010; Head of London and UK Wide Operations, Government Olympic Executive from 2010.

Tom Petzal (b. 1945) – Trustee 2004-11 (resigned 2011). Worked with the London Celebrations Committee as Co-ordinator of the varied Borough activities in London during the Silver Jubilee; recalled for a similar job in 2002. Of his work for the London Celebrations Committee, Lord Drogheda wrote: 'we recruited a young man, Tom Petzal, whose job it was to go round the boroughs and urge them to help and encourage local manifestations of loyalty, even the most republican of councillors finding him hard to withstand.'

John Polk (b. Washington, DC, 1942) – Trustee from 2006, Hon Treasurer from 2006. Worked in The City for 40 years at Lazard's, Clark Dodge, Brown Brothers Harriman, & A.G. Edwards; Trustee of Goodenough College, & Tower Hill Trust; Liveryman of Goldsmiths' Company.

3   THE SPONSORS

The Jubilee Walkway Trust was started with money from the London Celebrations Committee for The Queen's Silver Jubilee. Both routes were created and have been maintained by many generous sponsors. In particular we would like to thank the Greater London Authority, Transport for London, Royal Parks and all the managing authorities through which the routes pass. Over the years we received substantial grants from the Heritage Lottery Fund, the Corporation of London, Westminster City Council, the Civic Trust and in the early days the Greater London Council.

Individual panels were sponsored, maps were sponsored, and there was considerable support in kind. In a perfect world, all the sponsors would be listed here, but in 35 years of help, there is danger that one might be inadvertently omitted. So we take this opportunity to thank each and every one for helping us in our enjoyable task.

4   THE PANORAMIC PANELS

The Trust has been very well supported by the Royal Family, who unveiled numerous panels over the years. Of course not all accepted and attempts by Robert Shaw to invite the Queen Mother and the Princess of Wales ('a matter of time') came to nought. The Duke of Edinburgh was unable to unveil one on the South Bank in 1993, but joined The Queen to unveil the Diamond Wedding panel in Parliament Square in 2007. I myself failed with several actors when I first became Chairman. Not every chosen location was accepted. In 1992, for example, the Speaker of the House of Commons thought the Terrace of the House 'may not be the most suitable site for a panel in this area.'

But the following panoramic panels were unveiled on and about the Walkway:

1977
9 June – South Bank Lion plaque – HM The Queen.

1980
1 October – Lambeth Palace (PP) – Rt Rev Robert Runcie, Archbishop of Canterbury, who entertained the guests to sherry in the Old Guard Room of Lambeth Palace afterwards. He wrote later that he had 'the warmest feelings about the whole operation'.
7 October – Parliament Square – Norman Tebbit, Parliamentary Under-Secretary of State, Department of Trade and Industry.

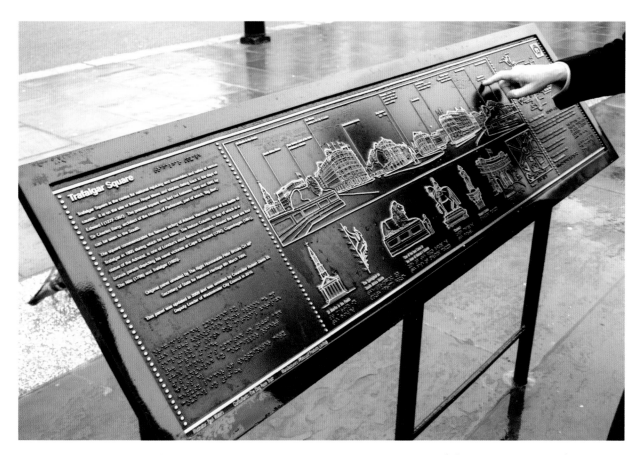

The panoramic panel in Trafalgar Square.

State, Department of the Environment and Minister for Sport.

1981
28 April – South Bank (Jubilee Gardens) – Bernard Brook-Partridge, Chairman of the GLC.
19 May – Bankside – Rt Hon Norman St John-Stevas.

1982
9 July – Tower Bridge – Sir Christopher Leaver, Lord Mayor of London.

1983
31 March – World Trade Centre – Sir Anthony Jolliffe, Lord Mayor of London.
31 May – Trafalgar Square (south west) – HRH The Duke of Gloucester (panel donated by the Government of Canada – subsequently stolen).
20 July – Trafalgar Square (north east) – Neil McFarlane, MP, Parliamentary Under Secretary of

1985
1 November – Tower Hill – HRH The Duke of Gloucester.

1987
16 September – Waterloo Bridge – Lord Brabazon of Tara.

1988
23 June – Victoria Embankment (opposite County Hall) – Lord Younger.
28 July – Old Thameside Inn – Sam Wanamaker.

1990
12 January – IBM Offices, Queen's Walk – Susan Hampshire.
14 June – Waterloo Bridge – Lady Sterling of Plaistow.

26 November – Parliament Square – Lord Tebbit (replacing the 1980 panel).

1991
16 January – Temple, Victoria Embankment – Rt Hon John Wakeham.
25 June – Hay's Wharf – Rt Hon Michael Heseltine, Secretary of State for the Environment.
23 July – Parliament Square (south side) – Viscount Ullswater, Minister for Tourism.

1992
27 May – Parliament Square (St Margaret's) – Viscount Tonypandy (commemorating 40th anniversary of The Queen's Accession).
4 June – Leicester Square landscape set piece – HM The Queen.

1993
9 June – London Bridge – HRH The Duke of Gloucester.
9 June – London Bridge – C. Douglas Woodward, Chief Commoner of the City of London.

1994
8 March – Trafalgar Square – Councillor Jenny Bianco, Lord Mayor of Westminster.
26 April – South Bank – Rt Hon John Gummer, Secretary of State for the Environment.
10 May – Lambeth Palace – Rt Rev John Yates, Bishop at Lambeth.
30 June – Tower Bridge – HRH The Prince of Wales.
1 November – St Clement Dane's – Ian Sproat, Under-Secretary of State for National Heritage.
10 November – London Bridge City – HM The Queen.
26 November – Rt Hon Stephen Dorrell, Secretary of State for National Heritage.

1996
12 July – Trafalgar Square – President Nelson Mandela of South Africa.

1998
28 April – Buckingham Palace – HRH The Duke of Gloucester (Golden Wedding panel).

2000
24 May – Cheapside – Robin Eve, Chief Commoner of the City of London (later destroyed).

2001
18 July – St Clement Dane's – Melanie Johnson MP, Minister for Competition, Consumers and Markets.

2002
30 April – Tower Hill Gardens – HRH The Duke of Gloucester.
31 May – Old Thameside Inn – Zoë Wanamaker.
11 June – Blackfriars Bridge – Sir Trevor McDonald.
12 June – Embankment – Baroness Boothroyd.
15 July – Parliament Square – Rt Hon Tessa Jowell.
24 October – One Poultry – HM The Queen.
3 December – London Bridge City – HRH The Duke of Gloucester.

2003
2 June – The Mall – HM The Queen.
8 July – Royal Exchange – The Lady Soames.
22 July – Leicester Square – Councillor Jan Prendergast, Lord Mayor of Westminster (removed in the renovation of Leicester Square, 2012).

2004
12 July – Trafalgar Square – HRH The Duke of Gloucester (in memory of Max Nicholson).

2007
17 January – HorseGuards Parade – HRH The Countess of Wessex (to mark the 80th Birthday of The Queen).
19 November – Parliament Square – HM The Queen & HRH The Duke of Edinburgh (Diamond Wedding Panel).

2010
30 November – Trafalgar Square – Councillor Robert Davis.

ABOVE   The Coin Street Rondel on The Queen's Walk.

LEFT   The Parliament Square Assembly Marker.

BELOW   The Rondel beside the London Eye.

5   THE PLAQUES AND RONDELS

There are two Walkway columns with the Jubilee crown on top – one on the way into Parliament Square from St James's Park (bearing a tribute to Neville Labovitch), and one on the South Bank near Jubilee Gardens.

1978

14 July – Chancery Lane plaque – HRH The Duke of Gloucester.

1979

3 October – Euston Station plaque – HRH The Duke of Gloucester.

1988

7 December – Rondel on The Queen's Walk – HM The Queen.

2001

8 March – Rondel by the London Eye – Ken Livingstone, Mayor of London.

2012

29 February – Jubilee Greenway disc outside Buckingham Palace – HM The Queen.

6   THE WALKWAY IN FILMS

Inevitably the Walkway makes occasional appearances in films. Ken Stott can be seen talking near one of the panels in an episode of *The Vice*. And in the Richard Curtis film, *The Boat that Rocks*, there is a clip of Westminster and Big Ben, which gives a fabulous view of the 2007 Parliament Square panel, before it got placed behind security fortifications. I always thought we should have persuaded the makers of the James Bond films to have their hero consult one of our panels to find his way. This would have been a good way to promote the usefulness of the walk.

There was also an early film made specifically on the Walkway by ILEA, and later a promotional video, with voice-over by Hugo Vickers, in 2004.

The Queen receiving The Queen's Jubilee Rose from Richard Beales at the Chelsea Flower Show, 21 May 2012.

7 AWARDS

1982 – Europa Nostra Award.
2005 – Best Community or Partnership Initiative, as part of the London Planning Awards.
2006 – A Civic Trust Mention.

8 TREES

1977 – Victoria Tower Gardens – Her Majesty The Queen.

2000 – St James's Park – HRH The Duke of Gloucester (Patron).
2005 – St Paul's Churchyard – Hugo Vickers (Chairman).
2011 – Chancery Lane – Hugo Vickers (Chairman).

9 THE QUEEN'S JUBILEE ROSE

In 2010 we had the idea of creating a new rose to ensure the Jubilee Greenway was well and truly 'green' and alive with colour and scent. We consulted Peter Beales Roses in Norfolk and they created a special classic rose named 'Queen's Jubilee Rose' – a repeat flowering scented white rose, flushed with peachy pink.

The Jubilee Greenway garden created by Peter Beales Roses, which won a Gold Medal at the Chelsea Flower Show in 2012.

We wanted to place the roses in the bouquets of winning athletes at the Olympic and Paralympic Games which got approval from everyone apart from the International Olympic Comittee who were concerned that white flowers were a negative symbol in some countries.

Nevertheless we decided to launch the new rose at the Chelsea Flower Show in 2012, where it was shortlisted for Plant of the Year by the Royal Horticultural Society. To illustrate how the Jubilee Greenway could look in the future for visitors to enjoy we loaned Walkway panels and commissioned three special Jubilee Greenway stands for Peter Beales to adorn the roses.

On 21 May Richard Beales presented a bouquet containing the new roses to The Queen when she visited the Flower Show. Our garden won a Gold Medal.

The rose was to be planted in the Buckingham Palace gardens, in the Olympic Park, and at other strategic points along the Jubilee Greenway.

Acknowledgements

I was fortunate to have access to the official archives of the Jubilee Walkway Trust, predating its inception in 1978, being the papers of Robert Shaw; also to the papers of Max Nicholson, relating to the work of the Environmental Committee of the London Celebrations Committee for The Queen's Silver Jubilee and the creation of the Walkway. The papers of the Trust included the working archives of the honorary secretary, Joyce Bellamy, and Fredi Newton, supplemented by papers belonging to Neville Labovitch, Chris Patey, Geoffrey Rowley and my own since 2000. As so often, I was able to refer back to private diaries I have kept, which fortunately added to something to accounts of the early days of the Walkway.

In conversations over many years I owe a huge debt to the late Max Nicholson himself, also to Sir James Swaffield, Jim Walker, Joyce Bellamy, and the present Trustees. I am indebted for further individual reminiscences to Chris Green, Press Officer to the London Celebrations Committee in 1977, and many more.

Photographs are from the collection of the Jubilee Walkway Trust. We are grateful to Elizabeth Vickers & Andy Johnson for photographs of the Jubilee Walkway, and to Elizabeth Vickers for the Jubilee Greenway images, all of which were specially taken for the Trust; some photographs additionally by David Hares, Hugo Vickers & Jim Walker.

Also to: Rex Features (pp. 24 & 97); John Sterling (p. 25); Maureen McLean (pp. 33, 56, 57, 58, & 119); Philip Hoare (p. 41).

Bibliography

Bagnold, Enid, *Enid Bagnold's Autobiography* (Heinemann, 1969)

Drogheda, Lord, *Double Harness – The Memoirs of Lord Drogheda* (Weidenfeld & Nicolson, 1978)

Fulford, Roger (ed), *Darling Child – Private Correspondence of Queen Victoria and the German Crown Princess, 1871-1878* (Evans Brothers, 1976)

Nicholson, Max, *The Silver Jubilee Walkway* (Civic Trust, 1977)
The System (Hodder & Stoughton, 1967)

Pope Hennessy, James, *History under Fire* Batsford, 1941)

Vickers, Hugo, *We Want The Queen* (Debrett, 1977)

Wales, HRH The Prince of, *A Vision of Britain* Doubleday, 1989)

Wright, Sir Paul, *A Brittle Glory* (Weidenfeld & Nicolson, 1986)

The National Archives, Foreign & Commonwealth Office papers, FCO 57/672, relating to the Silver Jubilee of 1977.

Real Life Crimes . . . and how they were solved, Volume 5, part 65 (The Vanishing Civil Servant) (Eaglemoss Publications, Ltd, 1995).